C-572 CAREER EXAMINATION SERIES

This is your
PASSBOOK for...

Parking Enforcement Agent

Test Preparation Study Guide
Questions & Answers

NATIONAL LEARNING CORPORATION®

COPYRIGHT NOTICE

This book is SOLELY intended for, is sold ONLY to, and its use is RESTRICTED to individual, bona fide applicants or candidates who qualify by virtue of having seriously filed applications for appropriate license, certificate, professional and/or promotional advancement, higher school matriculation, scholarship, or other legitimate requirements of education and/or governmental authorities.

This book is NOT intended for use, class instruction, tutoring, training, duplication, copying, reprinting, excerption, or adaptation, etc., by:

1) Other publishers
2) Proprietors and/or Instructors of "Coaching" and/or Preparatory Courses
3) Personnel and/or Training Divisions of commercial, industrial, and governmental organizations
4) Schools, colleges, or universities and/or their departments and staffs, including teachers and other personnel
5) Testing Agencies or Bureaus
6) Study groups which seek by the purchase of a single volume to copy and/or duplicate and/or adapt this material for use by the group as a whole without having purchased individual volumes for each of the members of the group
7) Et al.

Such persons would be in violation of appropriate Federal and State statutes.

PROVISION OF LICENSING AGREEMENTS – Recognized educational, commercial, industrial, and governmental institutions and organizations, and others legitimately engaged in educational pursuits, including training, testing, and measurement activities, may address request for a licensing agreement to the copyright owners, who will determine whether, and under what conditions, including fees and charges, the materials in this book may be used them. In other words, a licensing facility exists for the legitimate use of the material in this book on other than an individual basis. However, it is asseverated and affirmed here that the material in this book CANNOT be used without the receipt of the express permission of such a licensing agreement from the Publishers. Inquiries re licensing should be addressed to the company, attention rights and permissions department.

All rights reserved, including the right of reproduction in whole or in part, in any form or by any means, electronic or mechanical, including photocopying, recording, or by any information storage and retrieval system, without permission in writing from the Publisher.

Copyright © 2024 by
National Learning Corporation

212 Michael Drive, Syosset, NY 11791
(516) 921-8888 • www.passbooks.com
E-mail: info@passbooks.com

PASSBOOK® SERIES

THE *PASSBOOK® SERIES* has been created to prepare applicants and candidates for the ultimate academic battlefield – the examination room.

At some time in our lives, each and every one of us may be required to take an examination – for validation, matriculation, admission, qualification, registration, certification, or licensure.

Based on the assumption that every applicant or candidate has met the basic formal educational standards, has taken the required number of courses, and read the necessary texts, the *PASSBOOK® SERIES* furnishes the one special preparation which may assure passing with confidence, instead of failing with insecurity. Examination questions – together with answers – are furnished as the basic vehicle for study so that the mysteries of the examination and its compounding difficulties may be eliminated or diminished by a sure method.

This book is meant to help you pass your examination provided that you qualify and are serious in your objective.

The entire field is reviewed through the huge store of content information which is succinctly presented through a provocative and challenging approach – the question-and-answer method.

A climate of success is established by furnishing the correct answers at the end of each test.

You soon learn to recognize types of questions, forms of questions, and patterns of questioning. You may even begin to anticipate expected outcomes.

You perceive that many questions are repeated or adapted so that you can gain acute insights, which may enable you to score many sure points.

You learn how to confront new questions, or types of questions, and to attack them confidently and work out the correct answers.

You note objectives and emphases, and recognize pitfalls and dangers, so that you may make positive educational adjustments.

Moreover, you are kept fully informed in relation to new concepts, methods, practices, and directions in the field.

You discover that you are actually taking the examination all the time: you are preparing for the examination by "taking" an examination, not by reading extraneous and/or supererogatory textbooks.

In short, this PASSBOOK®, used directedly, should be an important factor in helping you to pass your test.

PARKING ENFORCEMENT AGENT

DUTIES AND RESPONSIBILITIES

Under direct supervision, patrols an assigned area and, as specifically empowered, enforces laws, rules and regulations relating to the parking, stopping and standing of vehicles; makes inspections of traffic conditions to regulate and control parking; removes foreign objects from parking meters; tests for timing defects; prepares and issues summonses for violations; records data regarding meter location, condition, and activities; operates motor vehicles; and perform related work.

EXAMPLES OF TYPICAL TASKS

Patrols, on foot, assigned areas and tickets vehicles, illegally parked, stopped, or standing, at meters, off-street parking metered areas, on the roadway side of any vehicle at the curb, within no-stopping and no-standing zones, where signs indicate the existence of such zones, in a bus stop or in a taxi stand zone where signs indicate the existence of such zones, and within a specified distance of a fire hydrant and on a roadway within a specified distance of the curb. Testifies in court relative to summonses issued. Determines whether commercial vehicles are liable to parking meter charges or summonses as required by the traffic regulations. Determines by visual and other inspection means whether meters are operating adequately. Reports inoperative or missing meters. Checks for meter feeding. Prepares court affidavits and required reports. Drives a passenger car or station wagon and operates a two-way radio in the vehicle to communicate with central office or area office.

TEST

The multiple-choice test may include questions on remembering new information; understanding the order in which to do things; understanding written language; communicating information to another person; recognizing the existence of a problem; applying general rules to a specific situation or identifying a common element in several different situations; recognizing where you are in relation to the space you are in and using a map or diagram to get from one position to another; standards of proper employee ethical conduct; and other related areas.

HOW TO TAKE A TEST

I. YOU MUST PASS AN EXAMINATION

A. *WHAT EVERY CANDIDATE SHOULD KNOW*

Examination applicants often ask us for help in preparing for the written test. What can I study in advance? What kinds of questions will be asked? How will the test be given? How will the papers be graded?

As an applicant for a civil service examination, you may be wondering about some of these things. Our purpose here is to suggest effective methods of advance study and to describe civil service examinations.

Your chances for success on this examination can be increased if you know how to prepare. Those "pre-examination jitters" can be reduced if you know what to expect. You can even experience an adventure in good citizenship if you know why civil service exams are given.

B. *WHY ARE CIVIL SERVICE EXAMINATIONS GIVEN?*

Civil service examinations are important to you in two ways. As a citizen, you want public jobs filled by employees who know how to do their work. As a job seeker, you want a fair chance to compete for that job on an equal footing with other candidates. The best-known means of accomplishing this two-fold goal is the competitive examination.

Exams are widely publicized throughout the nation. They may be administered for jobs in federal, state, city, municipal, town or village governments or agencies.

Any citizen may apply, with some limitations, such as the age or residence of applicants. Your experience and education may be reviewed to see whether you meet the requirements for the particular examination. When these requirements exist, they are reasonable and applied consistently to all applicants. Thus, a competitive examination may cause you some uneasiness now, but it is your privilege and safeguard.

C. *HOW ARE CIVIL SERVICE EXAMS DEVELOPED?*

Examinations are carefully written by trained technicians who are specialists in the field known as "psychological measurement," in consultation with recognized authorities in the field of work that the test will cover. These experts recommend the subject matter areas or skills to be tested; only those knowledges or skills important to your success on the job are included. The most reliable books and source materials available are used as references. Together, the experts and technicians judge the difficulty level of the questions.

Test technicians know how to phrase questions so that the problem is clearly stated. Their ethics do not permit "trick" or "catch" questions. Questions may have been tried out on sample groups, or subjected to statistical analysis, to determine their usefulness.

Written tests are often used in combination with performance tests, ratings of training and experience, and oral interviews. All of these measures combine to form the best-known means of finding the right person for the right job.

II. HOW TO PASS THE WRITTEN TEST

A. NATURE OF THE EXAMINATION

To prepare intelligently for civil service examinations, you should know how they differ from school examinations you have taken. In school you were assigned certain definite pages to read or subjects to cover. The examination questions were quite detailed and usually emphasized memory. Civil service exams, on the other hand, try to discover your present ability to perform the duties of a position, plus your potentiality to learn these duties. In other words, a civil service exam attempts to predict how successful you will be. Questions cover such a broad area that they cannot be as minute and detailed as school exam questions.

In the public service similar kinds of work, or positions, are grouped together in one "class." This process is known as *position-classification*. All the positions in a class are paid according to the salary range for that class. One class title covers all of these positions, and they are all tested by the same examination.

B. FOUR BASIC STEPS

1) Study the announcement

How, then, can you know what subjects to study? Our best answer is: "Learn as much as possible about the class of positions for which you've applied." The exam will test the knowledge, skills and abilities needed to do the work.

Your most valuable source of information about the position you want is the official exam announcement. This announcement lists the training and experience qualifications. Check these standards and apply only if you come reasonably close to meeting them.

The brief description of the position in the examination announcement offers some clues to the subjects which will be tested. Think about the job itself. Review the duties in your mind. Can you perform them, or are there some in which you are rusty? Fill in the blank spots in your preparation.

Many jurisdictions preview the written test in the exam announcement by including a section called "Knowledge and Abilities Required," "Scope of the Examination," or some similar heading. Here you will find out specifically what fields will be tested.

2) Review your own background

Once you learn in general what the position is all about, and what you need to know to do the work, ask yourself which subjects you already know fairly well and which need improvement. You may wonder whether to concentrate on improving your strong areas or on building some background in your fields of weakness. When the announcement has specified "some knowledge" or "considerable knowledge," or has used adjectives like "beginning principles of…" or "advanced … methods," you can get a clue as to the number and difficulty of questions to be asked in any given field. More questions, and hence broader coverage, would be included for those subjects which are more important in the work. Now weigh your strengths and weaknesses against the job requirements and prepare accordingly.

3) Determine the level of the position

Another way to tell how intensively you should prepare is to understand the level of the job for which you are applying. Is it the entering level? In other words, is this the position in which beginners in a field of work are hired? Or is it an intermediate or advanced level? Sometimes this is indicated by such words as "Junior" or "Senior" in the class title. Other jurisdictions use Roman numerals to designate the level – Clerk I, Clerk II, for example. The word "Supervisor" sometimes appears in the title. If the level is not indicated by the title, check the description of duties. Will you be working under very close supervision, or will you have responsibility for independent decisions in this work?

4) Choose appropriate study materials

Now that you know the subjects to be examined and the relative amount of each subject to be covered, you can choose suitable study materials. For beginning level jobs, or even advanced ones, if you have a pronounced weakness in some aspect of your training, read a modern, standard textbook in that field. Be sure it is up to date and has general coverage. Such books are normally available at your library, and the librarian will be glad to help you locate one. For entry-level positions, questions of appropriate difficulty are chosen – neither highly advanced questions, nor those too simple. Such questions require careful thought but not advanced training.

If the position for which you are applying is technical or advanced, you will read more advanced, specialized material. If you are already familiar with the basic principles of your field, elementary textbooks would waste your time. Concentrate on advanced textbooks and technical periodicals. Think through the concepts and review difficult problems in your field.

These are all general sources. You can get more ideas on your own initiative, following these leads. For example, training manuals and publications of the government agency which employs workers in your field can be useful, particularly for technical and professional positions. A letter or visit to the government department involved may result in more specific study suggestions, and certainly will provide you with a more definite idea of the exact nature of the position you are seeking.

III. KINDS OF TESTS

Tests are used for purposes other than measuring knowledge and ability to perform specified duties. For some positions, it is equally important to test ability to make adjustments to new situations or to profit from training. In others, basic mental abilities not dependent on information are essential. Questions which test these things may not appear as pertinent to the duties of the position as those which test for knowledge and information. Yet they are often highly important parts of a fair examination. For very general questions, it is almost impossible to help you direct your study efforts. What we can do is to point out some of the more common of these general abilities needed in public service positions and describe some typical questions.

1) General information

Broad, general information has been found useful for predicting job success in some kinds of work. This is tested in a variety of ways, from vocabulary lists to questions about current events. Basic background in some field of work, such as sociology or economics, may be sampled in a group of questions. Often these are principles which have become familiar to most persons through exposure rather than through formal training. It is difficult to advise you how to study for these questions; being alert to the world around you is our best suggestion.

2) Verbal ability

An example of an ability needed in many positions is verbal or language ability. Verbal ability is, in brief, the ability to use and understand words. Vocabulary and grammar tests are typical measures of this ability. Reading comprehension or paragraph interpretation questions are common in many kinds of civil service tests. You are given a paragraph of written material and asked to find its central meaning.

3) Numerical ability

Number skills can be tested by the familiar arithmetic problem, by checking paired lists of numbers to see which are alike and which are different, or by interpreting charts and graphs. In the latter test, a graph may be printed in the test booklet which you are asked to use as the basis for answering questions.

4) Observation

A popular test for law-enforcement positions is the observation test. A picture is shown to you for several minutes, then taken away. Questions about the picture test your ability to observe both details and larger elements.

5) Following directions

In many positions in the public service, the employee must be able to carry out written instructions dependably and accurately. You may be given a chart with several columns, each column listing a variety of information. The questions require you to carry out directions involving the information given in the chart.

6) Skills and aptitudes

Performance tests effectively measure some manual skills and aptitudes. When the skill is one in which you are trained, such as typing or shorthand, you can practice. These tests are often very much like those given in business school or high school courses. For many of the other skills and aptitudes, however, no short-time preparation can be made. Skills and abilities natural to you or that you have developed throughout your lifetime are being tested.

Many of the general questions just described provide all the data needed to answer the questions and ask you to use your reasoning ability to find the answers. Your best preparation for these tests, as well as for tests of facts and ideas, is to be at your physical and mental best. You, no doubt, have your own methods of getting into an exam-taking mood and keeping "in shape." The next section lists some ideas on this subject.

IV. KINDS OF QUESTIONS

Only rarely is the "essay" question, which you answer in narrative form, used in civil service tests. Civil service tests are usually of the short-answer type. Full instructions for answering these questions will be given to you at the examination. But in case this is your first experience with short-answer questions and separate answer sheets, here is what you need to know:

1) Multiple-choice Questions

Most popular of the short-answer questions is the "multiple choice" or "best answer" question. It can be used, for example, to test for factual knowledge, ability to solve problems or judgment in meeting situations found at work.

A multiple-choice question is normally one of three types—
- It can begin with an incomplete statement followed by several possible endings. You are to find the one ending which *best* completes the statement, although some of the others may not be entirely wrong.
- It can also be a complete statement in the form of a question which is answered by choosing one of the statements listed.

- It can be in the form of a problem – again you select the best answer.

Here is an example of a multiple-choice question with a discussion which should give you some clues as to the method for choosing the right answer:

When an employee has a complaint about his assignment, the action which will *best* help him overcome his difficulty is to
   A. discuss his difficulty with his coworkers
   B. take the problem to the head of the organization
   C. take the problem to the person who gave him the assignment
   D. say nothing to anyone about his complaint

In answering this question, you should study each of the choices to find which is best. Consider choice "A" – Certainly an employee may discuss his complaint with fellow employees, but no change or improvement can result, and the complaint remains unresolved. Choice "B" is a poor choice since the head of the organization probably does not know what assignment you have been given, and taking your problem to him is known as "going over the head" of the supervisor. The supervisor, or person who made the assignment, is the person who can clarify it or correct any injustice. Choice "C" is, therefore, correct. To say nothing, as in choice "D," is unwise. Supervisors have and interest in knowing the problems employees are facing, and the employee is seeking a solution to his problem.

2) True/False Questions

The "true/false" or "right/wrong" form of question is sometimes used. Here a complete statement is given. Your job is to decide whether the statement is right or wrong.

SAMPLE: A roaming cell-phone call to a nearby city costs less than a non-roaming call to a distant city.

This statement is wrong, or false, since roaming calls are more expensive.
This is not a complete list of all possible question forms, although most of the others are variations of these common types. You will always get complete directions for answering questions. Be sure you understand *how* to mark your answers – ask questions until you do.

V. RECORDING YOUR ANSWERS

Computer terminals are used more and more today for many different kinds of exams.
For an examination with very few applicants, you may be told to record your answers in the test booklet itself. Separate answer sheets are much more common. If this separate answer sheet is to be scored by machine – and this is often the case – it is highly important that you mark your answers correctly in order to get credit.

An electronic scoring machine is often used in civil service offices because of the speed with which papers can be scored. Machine-scored answer sheets must be marked with a pencil, which will be given to you. This pencil has a high graphite content which responds to the electronic scoring machine. As a matter of fact, stray dots may register as answers, so do not let your pencil rest on the answer sheet while you are pondering the correct answer. Also, if your pencil lead breaks or is otherwise defective, ask for another.

Since the answer sheet will be dropped in a slot in the scoring machine, be careful not to bend the corners or get the paper crumpled.

The answer sheet normally has five vertical columns of numbers, with 30 numbers to a column. These numbers correspond to the question numbers in your test booklet. After each number, going across the page are four or five pairs of dotted lines. These short dotted lines have small letters or numbers above them. The first two pairs may also have a "T" or "F" above the letters. This indicates that the first two pairs only are to be used if the questions are of the true-false type. If the questions are multiple choice, disregard the "T" and "F" and pay attention only to the small letters or numbers.

Answer your questions in the manner of the sample that follows:

32. The largest city in the United States is
    A. Washington, D.C.
    B. New York City
    C. Chicago
    D. Detroit
    E. San Francisco

1) Choose the answer you think is best. (New York City is the largest, so "B" is correct.)
2) Find the row of dotted lines numbered the same as the question you are answering. (Find row number 32)
3) Find the pair of dotted lines corresponding to the answer. (Find the pair of lines under the mark "B.")
4) Make a solid black mark between the dotted lines.

VI. BEFORE THE TEST

Common sense will help you find procedures to follow to get ready for an examination. Too many of us, however, overlook these sensible measures. Indeed, nervousness and fatigue have been found to be the most serious reasons why applicants fail to do their best on civil service tests. Here is a list of reminders:

- Begin your preparation early – Don't wait until the last minute to go scurrying around for books and materials or to find out what the position is all about.
- Prepare continuously – An hour a night for a week is better than an all-night cram session. This has been definitely established. What is more, a night a week for a month will return better dividends than crowding your study into a shorter period of time.
- Locate the place of the exam – You have been sent a notice telling you when and where to report for the examination. If the location is in a different town or otherwise unfamiliar to you, it would be well to inquire the best route and learn something about the building.
- Relax the night before the test – Allow your mind to rest. Do not study at all that night. Plan some mild recreation or diversion; then go to bed early and get a good night's sleep.
- Get up early enough to make a leisurely trip to the place for the test – This way unforeseen events, traffic snarls, unfamiliar buildings, etc. will not upset you.
- Dress comfortably – A written test is not a fashion show. You will be known by number and not by name, so wear something comfortable.

- Leave excess paraphernalia at home – Shopping bags and odd bundles will get in your way. You need bring only the items mentioned in the official notice you received; usually everything you need is provided. Do not bring reference books to the exam. They will only confuse those last minutes and be taken away from you when in the test room.
- Arrive somewhat ahead of time – If because of transportation schedules you must get there very early, bring a newspaper or magazine to take your mind off yourself while waiting.
- Locate the examination room – When you have found the proper room, you will be directed to the seat or part of the room where you will sit. Sometimes you are given a sheet of instructions to read while you are waiting. Do not fill out any forms until you are told to do so; just read them and be prepared.
- Relax and prepare to listen to the instructions
- If you have any physical problem that may keep you from doing your best, be sure to tell the test administrator. If you are sick or in poor health, you really cannot do your best on the exam. You can come back and take the test some other time.

VII. AT THE TEST

The day of the test is here and you have the test booklet in your hand. The temptation to get going is very strong. Caution! There is more to success than knowing the right answers. You must know how to identify your papers and understand variations in the type of short-answer question used in this particular examination. Follow these suggestions for maximum results from your efforts:

1) Cooperate with the monitor
The test administrator has a duty to create a situation in which you can be as much at ease as possible. He will give instructions, tell you when to begin, check to see that you are marking your answer sheet correctly, and so on. He is not there to guard you, although he will see that your competitors do not take unfair advantage. He wants to help you do your best.

2) Listen to all instructions
Don't jump the gun! Wait until you understand all directions. In most civil service tests you get more time than you need to answer the questions. So don't be in a hurry. Read each word of instructions until you clearly understand the meaning. Study the examples, listen to all announcements and follow directions. Ask questions if you do not understand what to do.

3) Identify your papers
Civil service exams are usually identified by number only. You will be assigned a number; you must not put your name on your test papers. Be sure to copy your number correctly. Since more than one exam may be given, copy your exact examination title.

4) Plan your time
Unless you are told that a test is a "speed" or "rate of work" test, speed itself is usually not important. Time enough to answer all the questions will be provided, but this does not mean that you have all day. An overall time limit has been set. Divide the total time (in minutes) by the number of questions to determine the approximate time you have for each question.

5) Do not linger over difficult questions
If you come across a difficult question, mark it with a paper clip (useful to have along) and come back to it when you have been through the booklet. One caution if you do this – be sure to skip a number on your answer sheet as well. Check often to be sure that you have not lost your place and that you are marking in the row numbered the same as the question you are answering.

6) Read the questions
Be sure you know what the question asks! Many capable people are unsuccessful because they failed to *read* the questions correctly.

7) Answer all questions
Unless you have been instructed that a penalty will be deducted for incorrect answers, it is better to guess than to omit a question.

8) Speed tests
It is often better NOT to guess on speed tests. It has been found that on timed tests people are tempted to spend the last few seconds before time is called in marking answers at random – without even reading them – in the hope of picking up a few extra points. To discourage this practice, the instructions may warn you that your score will be "corrected" for guessing. That is, a penalty will be applied. The incorrect answers will be deducted from the correct ones, or some other penalty formula will be used.

9) Review your answers
If you finish before time is called, go back to the questions you guessed or omitted to give them further thought. Review other answers if you have time.

10) Return your test materials
If you are ready to leave before others have finished or time is called, take ALL your materials to the monitor and leave quietly. Never take any test material with you. The monitor can discover whose papers are not complete, and taking a test booklet may be grounds for disqualification.

VIII. EXAMINATION TECHNIQUES

1) Read the general instructions carefully. These are usually printed on the first page of the exam booklet. As a rule, these instructions refer to the timing of the examination; the fact that you should not start work until the signal and must stop work at a signal, etc. If there are any *special* instructions, such as a choice of questions to be answered, make sure that you note this instruction carefully.

2) When you are ready to start work on the examination, that is as soon as the signal has been given, read the instructions to each question booklet, underline any key words or phrases, such as *least, best, outline, describe* and the like. In this way you will tend to answer as requested rather than discover on reviewing your paper that you *listed without describing*, that you selected the *worst* choice rather than the *best* choice, etc.

3) If the examination is of the objective or multiple-choice type – that is, each question will also give a series of possible answers: A, B, C or D, and you are called upon to select the best answer and write the letter next to that answer on your answer paper – it is advisable to start answering each question in turn. There may be anywhere from 50 to 100 such questions in the three or four hours allotted and you can see how much time would be taken if you read through all the questions before beginning to answer any. Furthermore, if you come across a question or group of questions which you know would be difficult to answer, it would undoubtedly affect your handling of all the other questions.

4) If the examination is of the essay type and contains but a few questions, it is a moot point as to whether you should read all the questions before starting to answer any one. Of course, if you are given a choice – say five out of seven and the like – then it is essential to read all the questions so you can eliminate the two that are most difficult. If, however, you are asked to answer all the questions, there may be danger in trying to answer the easiest one first because you may find that you will spend too much time on it. The best technique is to answer the first question, then proceed to the second, etc.

5) Time your answers. Before the exam begins, write down the time it started, then add the time allowed for the examination and write down the time it must be completed, then divide the time available somewhat as follows:
    - If 3-1/2 hours are allowed, that would be 210 minutes. If you have 80 objective-type questions, that would be an average of 2-1/2 minutes per question. Allow yourself no more than 2 minutes per question, or a total of 160 minutes, which will permit about 50 minutes to review.
    - If for the time allotment of 210 minutes there are 7 essay questions to answer, that would average about 30 minutes a question. Give yourself only 25 minutes per question so that you have about 35 minutes to review.

6) The most important instruction is to *read each question* and make sure you know what is wanted. The second most important instruction is to *time yourself properly* so that you answer every question. The third most important instruction is to *answer every question*. Guess if you have to but include something for each question. Remember that you will receive no credit for a blank and will probably receive some credit if you write something in answer to an essay question. If you guess a letter – say "B" for a multiple-choice question – you may have guessed right. If you leave a blank as an answer to a multiple-choice question, the examiners may respect your feelings but it will not add a point to your score. Some exams may penalize you for wrong answers, so in such cases *only*, you may not want to guess unless you have some basis for your answer.

7) Suggestions
    a. Objective-type questions
        1. Examine the question booklet for proper sequence of pages and questions
        2. Read all instructions carefully
        3. Skip any question which seems too difficult; return to it after all other questions have been answered
        4. Apportion your time properly; do not spend too much time on any single question or group of questions

5. Note and underline key words – *all, most, fewest, least, best, worst, same, opposite,* etc.
6. Pay particular attention to negatives
7. Note unusual option, e.g., unduly long, short, complex, different or similar in content to the body of the question
8. Observe the use of "hedging" words – *probably, may, most likely,* etc.
9. Make sure that your answer is put next to the same number as the question
10. Do not second-guess unless you have good reason to believe the second answer is definitely more correct
11. Cross out original answer if you decide another answer is more accurate; do not erase until you are ready to hand your paper in
12. Answer all questions; guess unless instructed otherwise
13. Leave time for review

b. Essay questions
   1. Read each question carefully
   2. Determine exactly what is wanted. Underline key words or phrases.
   3. Decide on outline or paragraph answer
   4. Include many different points and elements unless asked to develop any one or two points or elements
   5. Show impartiality by giving pros and cons unless directed to select one side only
   6. Make and write down any assumptions you find necessary to answer the questions
   7. Watch your English, grammar, punctuation and choice of words
   8. Time your answers; don't crowd material

8) Answering the essay question

Most essay questions can be answered by framing the specific response around several key words or ideas. Here are a few such key words or ideas:

M's: manpower, materials, methods, money, management
P's: purpose, program, policy, plan, procedure, practice, problems, pitfalls, personnel, public relations

   a. Six basic steps in handling problems:
      1. Preliminary plan and background development
      2. Collect information, data and facts
      3. Analyze and interpret information, data and facts
      4. Analyze and develop solutions as well as make recommendations
      5. Prepare report and sell recommendations
      6. Install recommendations and follow up effectiveness

   b. Pitfalls to avoid
      1. *Taking things for granted* – A statement of the situation does not necessarily imply that each of the elements is necessarily true; for example, a complaint may be invalid and biased so that all that can be taken for granted is that a complaint has been registered

2. *Considering only one side of a situation* – Wherever possible, indicate several alternatives and then point out the reasons you selected the best one
3. *Failing to indicate follow up* – Whenever your answer indicates action on your part, make certain that you will take proper follow-up action to see how successful your recommendations, procedures or actions turn out to be
4. *Taking too long in answering any single question* – Remember to time your answers properly

IX. AFTER THE TEST

Scoring procedures differ in detail among civil service jurisdictions although the general principles are the same. Whether the papers are hand-scored or graded by machine we have described, they are nearly always graded by number. That is, the person who marks the paper knows only the number – never the name – of the applicant. Not until all the papers have been graded will they be matched with names. If other tests, such as training and experience or oral interview ratings have been given, scores will be combined. Different parts of the examination usually have different weights. For example, the written test might count 60 percent of the final grade, and a rating of training and experience 40 percent. In many jurisdictions, veterans will have a certain number of points added to their grades.

After the final grade has been determined, the names are placed in grade order and an eligible list is established. There are various methods for resolving ties between those who get the same final grade – probably the most common is to place first the name of the person whose application was received first. Job offers are made from the eligible list in the order the names appear on it. You will be notified of your grade and your rank as soon as all these computations have been made. This will be done as rapidly as possible.

People who are found to meet the requirements in the announcement are called "eligibles." Their names are put on a list of eligible candidates. An eligible's chances of getting a job depend on how high he stands on this list and how fast agencies are filling jobs from the list.

When a job is to be filled from a list of eligibles, the agency asks for the names of people on the list of eligibles for that job. When the civil service commission receives this request, it sends to the agency the names of the three people highest on this list. Or, if the job to be filled has specialized requirements, the office sends the agency the names of the top three persons who meet these requirements from the general list.

The appointing officer makes a choice from among the three people whose names were sent to him. If the selected person accepts the appointment, the names of the others are put back on the list to be considered for future openings.

That is the rule in hiring from all kinds of eligible lists, whether they are for typist, carpenter, chemist, or something else. For every vacancy, the appointing officer has his choice of any one of the top three eligibles on the list. This explains why the person whose name is on top of the list sometimes does not get an appointment when some of the persons lower on the list do. If the appointing officer chooses the second or third eligible, the No. 1 eligible does not get a job at once, but stays on the list until he is appointed or the list is terminated.

X. HOW TO PASS THE INTERVIEW TEST

The examination for which you applied requires an oral interview test. You have already taken the written test and you are now being called for the interview test – the final part of the formal examination.

You may think that it is not possible to prepare for an interview test and that there are no procedures to follow during an interview. Our purpose is to point out some things you can do in advance that will help you and some good rules to follow and pitfalls to avoid while you are being interviewed.

What is an interview supposed to test?

The written examination is designed to test the technical knowledge and competence of the candidate; the oral is designed to evaluate intangible qualities, not readily measured otherwise, and to establish a list showing the relative fitness of each candidate – as measured against his competitors – for the position sought. Scoring is not on the basis of "right" and "wrong," but on a sliding scale of values ranging from "not passable" to "outstanding." As a matter of fact, it is possible to achieve a relatively low score without a single "incorrect" answer because of evident weakness in the qualities being measured.

Occasionally, an examination may consist entirely of an oral test – either an individual or a group oral. In such cases, information is sought concerning the technical knowledges and abilities of the candidate, since there has been no written examination for this purpose. More commonly, however, an oral test is used to supplement a written examination.

Who conducts interviews?

The composition of oral boards varies among different jurisdictions. In nearly all, a representative of the personnel department serves as chairman. One of the members of the board may be a representative of the department in which the candidate would work. In some cases, "outside experts" are used, and, frequently, a businessman or some other representative of the general public is asked to serve. Labor and management or other special groups may be represented. The aim is to secure the services of experts in the appropriate field.

However the board is composed, it is a good idea (and not at all improper or unethical) to ascertain in advance of the interview who the members are and what groups they represent. When you are introduced to them, you will have some idea of their backgrounds and interests, and at least you will not stutter and stammer over their names.

What should be done before the interview?

While knowledge about the board members is useful and takes some of the surprise element out of the interview, there is other preparation which is more substantive. It *is* possible to prepare for an oral interview – in several ways:

1) Keep a copy of your application and review it carefully before the interview

This may be the only document before the oral board, and the starting point of the interview. Know what education and experience you have listed there, and the sequence and dates of all of it. Sometimes the board will ask you to review the highlights of your experience for them; you should not have to hem and haw doing it.

2) Study the class specification and the examination announcement

Usually, the oral board has one or both of these to guide them. The qualities, characteristics or knowledges required by the position sought are stated in these documents. They offer valuable clues as to the nature of the oral interview. For example, if the job involves supervisory responsibilities, the announcement will usually indicate that knowledge of modern supervisory methods and the qualifications of the candidate as a supervisor will be tested. If so, you can expect such questions, frequently in the form of a hypothetical situation which you are expected to solve. NEVER go into an oral without knowledge of the duties and responsibilities of the job you seek.

3) Think through each qualification required

Try to visualize the kind of questions you would ask if you were a board member. How well could you answer them? Try especially to appraise your own knowledge and background in each area, *measured against the job sought*, and identify any areas in which you are weak. Be critical and realistic – do not flatter yourself.

4) Do some general reading in areas in which you feel you may be weak

For example, if the job involves supervision and your past experience has NOT, some general reading in supervisory methods and practices, particularly in the field of human relations, might be useful. Do NOT study agency procedures or detailed manuals. The oral board will be testing your understanding and capacity, not your memory.

5) Get a good night's sleep and watch your general health and mental attitude

You will want a clear head at the interview. Take care of a cold or any other minor ailment, and of course, no hangovers.

What should be done on the day of the interview?

Now comes the day of the interview itself. Give yourself plenty of time to get there. Plan to arrive somewhat ahead of the scheduled time, particularly if your appointment is in the fore part of the day. If a previous candidate fails to appear, the board might be ready for you a bit early. By early afternoon an oral board is almost invariably behind schedule if there are many candidates, and you may have to wait. Take along a book or magazine to read, or your application to review, but leave any extraneous material in the waiting room when you go in for your interview. In any event, relax and compose yourself.

The matter of dress is important. The board is forming impressions about you – from your experience, your manners, your attitude, and your appearance. Give your personal appearance careful attention. Dress your best, but not your flashiest. Choose conservative, appropriate clothing, and be sure it is immaculate. This is a business interview, and your appearance should indicate that you regard it as such. Besides, being well groomed and properly dressed will help boost your confidence.

Sooner or later, someone will call your name and escort you into the interview room. *This is it.* From here on you are on your own. It is too late for any more preparation. But remember, you asked for this opportunity to prove your fitness, and you are here because your request was granted.

What happens when you go in?

The usual sequence of events will be as follows: The clerk (who is often the board stenographer) will introduce you to the chairman of the oral board, who will introduce you to the other members of the board. Acknowledge the introductions before you sit down. Do not be surprised if you find a microphone facing you or a stenotypist sitting by. Oral interviews are usually recorded in the event of an appeal or other review.

Usually the chairman of the board will open the interview by reviewing the highlights of your education and work experience from your application – primarily for the benefit of the other members of the board, as well as to get the material into the record. Do not interrupt or comment unless there is an error or significant misinterpretation; if that is the case, do not hesitate. But do not quibble about insignificant matters. Also, he will usually ask you some question about your education, experience or your present job – partly to get you to start talking and to establish the interviewing "rapport." He may start the actual questioning, or turn it over to one of the other members. Frequently, each member undertakes the questioning on a particular area, one in which he is perhaps most competent, so you can expect each member to participate in the examination. Because time is limited, you may also expect some rather abrupt switches in the direction the questioning takes, so do not be upset by it. Normally, a board member will not pursue a single line of questioning unless he discovers a particular strength or weakness.

After each member has participated, the chairman will usually ask whether any member has any further questions, then will ask you if you have anything you wish to add. Unless you are expecting this question, it may floor you. Worse, it may start you off on an extended, extemporaneous speech. The board is not usually seeking more information. The question is principally to offer you a last opportunity to present further qualifications or to indicate that you have nothing to add. So, if you feel that a significant qualification or characteristic has been overlooked, it is proper to point it out in a sentence or so. Do not compliment the board on the thoroughness of their examination – they have been sketchy, and you know it. If you wish, merely say, "No thank you, I have nothing further to add." This is a point where you can "talk yourself out" of a good impression or fail to present an important bit of information. Remember, *you close the interview yourself*.

The chairman will then say, "That is all, Mr. _____, thank you." Do not be startled; the interview is over, and quicker than you think. Thank him, gather your belongings and take your leave. Save your sigh of relief for the other side of the door.

How to put your best foot forward

Throughout this entire process, you may feel that the board individually and collectively is trying to pierce your defenses, seek out your hidden weaknesses and embarrass and confuse you. Actually, this is not true. They are obliged to make an appraisal of your qualifications for the job you are seeking, and they want to see you in your best light. Remember, they must interview all candidates and a non-cooperative candidate may become a failure in spite of their best efforts to bring out his qualifications. Here are 15 suggestions that will help you:

1) Be natural – Keep your attitude confident, not cocky

If you are not confident that you can do the job, do not expect the board to be. Do not apologize for your weaknesses, try to bring out your strong points. The board is interested in a positive, not negative, presentation. Cockiness will antagonize any board member and make him wonder if you are covering up a weakness by a false show of strength.

2) Get comfortable, but don't lounge or sprawl

Sit erectly but not stiffly. A careless posture may lead the board to conclude that you are careless in other things, or at least that you are not impressed by the importance of the occasion. Either conclusion is natural, even if incorrect. Do not fuss with your clothing, a pencil or an ashtray. Your hands may occasionally be useful to emphasize a point; do not let them become a point of distraction.

3) Do not wisecrack or make small talk

This is a serious situation, and your attitude should show that you consider it as such. Further, the time of the board is limited – they do not want to waste it, and neither should you.

4) Do not exaggerate your experience or abilities
In the first place, from information in the application or other interviews and sources, the board may know more about you than you think. Secondly, you probably will not get away with it. An experienced board is rather adept at spotting such a situation, so do not take the chance.

5) If you know a board member, do not make a point of it, yet do not hide it
Certainly you are not fooling him, and probably not the other members of the board. Do not try to take advantage of your acquaintanceship – it will probably do you little good.

6) Do not dominate the interview
Let the board do that. They will give you the clues – do not assume that you have to do all the talking. Realize that the board has a number of questions to ask you, and do not try to take up all the interview time by showing off your extensive knowledge of the answer to the first one.

7) Be attentive
You only have 20 minutes or so, and you should keep your attention at its sharpest throughout. When a member is addressing a problem or question to you, give him your undivided attention. Address your reply principally to him, but do not exclude the other board members.

8) Do not interrupt
A board member may be stating a problem for you to analyze. He will ask you a question when the time comes. Let him state the problem, and wait for the question.

9) Make sure you understand the question
Do not try to answer until you are sure what the question is. If it is not clear, restate it in your own words or ask the board member to clarify it for you. However, do not haggle about minor elements.

10) Reply promptly but not hastily
A common entry on oral board rating sheets is "candidate responded readily," or "candidate hesitated in replies." Respond as promptly and quickly as you can, but do not jump to a hasty, ill-considered answer.

11) Do not be peremptory in your answers
A brief answer is proper – but do not fire your answer back. That is a losing game from your point of view. The board member can probably ask questions much faster than you can answer them.

12) Do not try to create the answer you think the board member wants
He is interested in what kind of mind you have and how it works – not in playing games. Furthermore, he can usually spot this practice and will actually grade you down on it.

13) Do not switch sides in your reply merely to agree with a board member
Frequently, a member will take a contrary position merely to draw you out and to see if you are willing and able to defend your point of view. Do not start a debate, yet do not surrender a good position. If a position is worth taking, it is worth defending.

14) Do not be afraid to admit an error in judgment if you are shown to be wrong

The board knows that you are forced to reply without any opportunity for careful consideration. Your answer may be demonstrably wrong. If so, admit it and get on with the interview.

15) Do not dwell at length on your present job

The opening question may relate to your present assignment. Answer the question but do not go into an extended discussion. You are being examined for a *new* job, not your present one. As a matter of fact, try to phrase ALL your answers in terms of the job for which you are being examined.

Basis of Rating

Probably you will forget most of these "do's" and "don'ts" when you walk into the oral interview room. Even remembering them all will not ensure you a passing grade. Perhaps you did not have the qualifications in the first place. But remembering them will help you to put your best foot forward, without treading on the toes of the board members.

Rumor and popular opinion to the contrary notwithstanding, an oral board wants you to make the best appearance possible. They know you are under pressure – but they also want to see how you respond to it as a guide to what your reaction would be under the pressures of the job you seek. They will be influenced by the degree of poise you display, the personal traits you show and the manner in which you respond.

ABOUT THIS BOOK

This book contains tests divided into Examination Sections. Go through each test, answering every question in the margin. We have also attached a sample answer sheet at the back of the book that can be removed and used. At the end of each test look at the answer key and check your answers. On the ones you got wrong, look at the right answer choice and learn. Do not fill in the answers first. Do not memorize the questions and answers, but understand the answer and principles involved. On your test, the questions will likely be different from the samples. Questions are changed and new ones added. If you understand these past questions you should have success with any changes that arise. Tests may consist of several types of questions. We have additional books on each subject should more study be advisable or necessary for you. Finally, the more you study, the better prepared you will be. This book is intended to be the last thing you study before you walk into the examination room. Prior study of relevant texts is also recommended. NLC publishes some of these in our Fundamental Series. Knowledge and good sense are important factors in passing your exam. Good luck also helps. So now study this Passbook, absorb the material contained within and take that knowledge into the examination. Then do your best to pass that exam.

EXAMINATION SECTION

EXAMINATION SECTION
TEST 1

DIRECTIONS: Each question or incomplete statement is followed by several suggested answers or completions. Select the one that BEST answers the question or completes the statement. *PRINT THE LETTER OF THE CORRECT ANSWER IN THE SPACE AT THE RIGHT.*

Questions 1-6.

DIRECTIONS: Questions 1 through 6 are based on the following reading passage covering PROCEDURES FOR PATROL. When answering these questions, refer to this passage.

PROCEDURES FOR PATROL

The primary function of all Parking Enforcement Agents assigned to patrol duty shall be to patrol assigned areas and issue summonses to violators of various sections of the City Traffic Regulations, which sections govern the parking or operation of vehicles. Parking Enforcement Agents occasionally may be called upon to distribute educational pamphlets and perform other work, at the discretion of the Bureau Chief.

Each Agent on patrol duty will be assigned a certain area (or areas) to be patrolled each day. These areas will be assigned during the daily roll call. Walking Cards will describe the street locations of the patrol and the manner in which the patrol is to be walked.

A Traffic Department vehicle will be provided for daily patrol assignments when necessary. Each Agent shall accomplish an assigned field patrol in the following manner:
  a. Start each patrol at the location specified on the daily patrol sheet, and proceed as per walking instructions.
  b. Approach each metered space being utilized (each metered space in which a vehicle is parked). If the meter shows the expired flag, the member of the force shall prepare and affix a summons to the vehicle parked at meter.
  c. Any vehicle in violation of any regulation governing the parking, standing, stopping, or movement of vehicles will be issued a summons.
  d. No summons will be issued to a vehicle displaying an authorized vehicle identification plate of the Police Department unless the vehicle is parked in violation of the No Standing, No Stopping, Hydrant, Bus Stop, or Double Parking Regulations. Identification plates for Police Department automobiles are made of plastic and are of rectangular shape, 10 3/4" long, 3 3/4" high, black letters and numerals on a white background. The words "POLICE DEPT." are printed on the face with the identification number. In addition, the Police Department emblem is printed on each card. Identification plates for private automobiles are the same size and shape as those used on Police Department automobiles.

An Agent on patrol, when observing a person "feeding" a street meter (placing an additional coin in a meter so as to leave the vehicle parked for an additional period) shall prepare and affix a summons to the vehicle.

An Agent on patrol shall note on a computer card each missing or defective, out of order, or otherwise damaged meter.

1. Of the following, the work which the Parking Enforcement Agent performs MOST often is

    A. issuing summonses for parking violations
    B. distributing educational pamphlets
    C. assisting the Bureau Chief
    D. driving a City vehicle

2. The area to be covered by a Parking Enforcemeng Agent on patrol is

    A. determined by the Police Department
    B. regulated by the City Traffic Regulations
    C. marked off with red flags
    D. described on Walking Cards

3. A Parking Enforcement Agent reports a broken meter by

    A. issuing a summons
    B. making a mark on a computer card
    C. raising the flag on the broken meter
    D. attending a daily roll call

4. With respect to the use of an automobile for patrol duty,

    A. Parking Enforcement Agents must supply their own cars for patrol
    B. automobiles for patrol will be supplied by the Police Department
    C. Parking Enforcement Agents are permitted to park in a bus stop
    D. department vehicles will be provided when required for patrol

5. Parking Enforcement Agents sometimes issue summonses to drivers for "feeding" a street meter in violation of parking regulations. Which one of the following situations describes such a violation? A driver

    A. has moved from one metered space to another
    B. has parked next to a Police Department No Standing sign
    C. is parked by a meter which shows 30 minutes time still remaining
    D. has used a coin to reset the meter after his first time period expired

6. Vehicles displaying an authorized vehicle identification plate of the Police Department are allowed to park at expired meters. Which one of the following statements describes the proper size of identification plates for *private automobiles used for police work*? They

    A. are 10 3/4" long, and 3 3/4" high
    B. have white letters and numerals on a black background
    C. are 3 3/4" long, and 10 3/4" high
    D. have black letters and numerals on a white background

7. If a parking enforcement agent is questioned by an angry driver who has just been given a summons for violation of a parking regulation, which one of the following replies by the agent would be MOST likely to retain the good will of the complaining driver?

    A. "Let me explain as best I can the reasons for my action."
    B. "I'm only doing the job I'm getting paid for, so don't get mad at me."
    C. "I don't make the parking regulations, I just have to uphold them."
    D. "The City's rules and regulations are made to be obeyed by everyone."

8. One day, during the absence of her regular supervisor, a temporary supervisor assigns Jane Brown to a patrol car that she has worked before, but instructs her to carry out this assignment in a way which is different from her usual instructions.
Which one of the following actions BEST fulfills Agent Brown's responsibility as a parking enforcement agent?

   A. Follow the instructions of her temporary supervisor without comment
   B. Explain to this supervisor how this work has been done in the past
   C. If she thinks that past instructions were better, Brown should disregard any new instructions
   D. Ask the other agents what they are going, and follow their lead

9. Parking enforcement agents should wear their badges only when in uniform or as ordered by the bureau chief. The badge must be displayed on the agent's outermost uniform garment on the area provided for the badge. An agent must immediately report the loss of a badge to the district commander, and must also submit a statement of the events leading up to the loss. The agent who lost the badge must pay for a new one.
According to the paragraph above, one of the rules concerning the wearing of the badge by a parking enforcement agent is that

   A. the badge must be worn on the inside coat pocket at all times
   B. a temporary badge should be borrowed to replace a lost badge
   C. the badge must be worn where it can be seen on the uniform
   D. only bureau chiefs and district commanders are required to wear badges

10. As required by the traffic bureau's uniform specifications, parking enforcement agents must purchase their own uniforms. Uniforms appropriate for seasonal use must be displayed at semi-annual inspections. An annual uniform allowance is granted to all members of the force to cover the cost of their uniforms.
According to the paragraph above, one of the rules concerning the purchase of uniforms is that

   A. the traffic bureau supplies uniforms to all parking enforcement agents
   B. parking enforcement agents are required to purchase their own uniforms
   C. parking enforcement agents only wear uniforms for semi-annual inspections
   D. parking enforcement agents select their own uniform colors

11. Inspection of uniforms is conducted in the parking enforcement agent's field office. Regular uniform inspection is held as follows:
   The winter uniform is inspected in May, and includes rain gear, jacket, overcoat, hat, skirt or trousers, shoes, boots (optional), ties (2), hood, shoulder bag, and gloves.
   The summer uniform, is inspected in January and includes rain gear, suit, cap, and gloves.
According to the paragraph above, which one of the following lists contains the categories of uniform items which are included in both the winter and summer inspections?

   A. Shoes and gloves
   B. Suit, cap, and shoulder bag
   C. Rain gear, jacket, and overcoat
   D. Gloves and rain gear

12. When reporting for duty, a parking enforcement agent who is assigned to operate a department of traffic motor vehicle must carefully inspect the vehicle to see that it is in serviceable condition. When making the inspection, the operator must check to see that
    sufficient gasoline is in the tank and the proper amount of oil in the crankcase;
    the radiator is properly filled with water, and, when department orders require, sufficient anti-freeze is maintained in the radiator;
    brakes, lights, windshield wipers, and warning devices are working properly;
    tires, and spare, are properly inflated.
    According to the paragraph above, it is the responsibility of the operator of a department motor vehicle, before taking it on the road, to check the condition of the

    A. tires   B. engine   C. transmission   D. battery

13. A parking enforcement agent's immediate supervisor is the *BEST* source of information on the duties and responsibilities of the job. According to the procedures of the traffic control bureau:
    The chain of authority for the uniformed force shall be in the following order: Commissioner; bureau chief; assistant bureau chief; regional commander; district commander; squad leader; parking enforcement agent.
    Based on the procedure above, whom should a parking enforcement agent ask for help in filling out a daily report? The

    A. regional commander   B. squad leader
    C. bureau chief   D. district commander

14. According to the procedures of the traffic control bureau:
    A parking enforcement agent shall follow all lawful verbal and written instructions, policies, procedures, and any other directions of a superior officer;
    promptly inform a superior officer of any unusual occurrences; take no action involving physical force against any individual and, shall at all times, act in a manner which will further the aims of the city, the department, and the bureau.
    Based on the procedures above, what is the proper action to be taken by a parking enforcement agent upon observing what appears to be a robbery in progress?

    A. Watch everything that happens and make notes for a daily report
    B. Report the incident to a superior officer by the nearest telephone
    C. Assist the apparent victims to repel their attackers
    D. Continue on the assigned patrol, maintaining the normal schedule

Questions 15-20.

DIRECTIONS: Questions 15 through 20 are based on the following reading passage covering the OPERATION OF DEPARTMENT MOTOR VEHICLES. When answering these questions, refer to this passage.

OPERATION OF DEPARTMENT MOTOR VEHICLES

When operating a Traffic Department motor vehicle, a member of the force must show every courtesy to other drivers, obey all traffic signs and traffic regulations, obey all other lawful authority, and handle the vehicle in a manner which will foster safety practices in others and create a favorable impression of the Bureau, the Department, and the City. The operator and passengers must use the safety belts.

Driving Rules -
- a. *Do not* operate a mechanically defective vehicle.
   Do not race engine on starting.
   Do not tamper with mechanical equipment.
   Do not run engine if there is an indication of low engine oil pressure, overheating, or no transmission oil.
- b. When parking on highway, all safety precautions must be observed.
- c. When parking in a garage or parking field, observe a maximum speed of 5 miles per hour. Place shift lever in park or neutral position, effectively apply hand brake, then shut off all ignition and light switches to prevent excess battery drain, and close all windows.

Reporting Defects -
- a. Report all observed defects on Drivers' Vehicle Defect Card and on Monthly Vehicle Report Form 49 in sufficient detail so a mechanic can easily locate the source of trouble.
- b. Enter vehicle road service calls and actual time of occurrence on Monthly Vehicle Report.

Reporting Accidents -
Promptly report all facts of each accident as follows: For serious accidents, including those involving personal injury, call your supervisor as soon as possible. Give all the appropriate information about the accident to your supervisor.

Record vehicle registration information, including the name of the registered owner, the state, year, and serial number, and the classification marking on the license plates. Also record the operator's license number and other identifying information, and, if it applies, the injured person's age and sex.

Give a full description of how the accident happened, and what happened following the accident, including the vehicles in collision, witnesses, police badge number, hospital, condition of road surface, time of day, weather conditions, location (near, far, center of intersection), and damage.

Repairs to Automobiles -
When a Department motor vehicle requires repairs that cannot be made by the operator, or requires replacement of parts or accessories (including tires and tubes), or requires towing, the operator shall notify the District Commander.

When a Departmental motor vehicle is placed out of service for repairs, the Regional Commander shall assign another vehicle, if available.

Daily Operator's Report -
The operator of a Department automobile shall keep a daily maintenance record of the vehicle, and note any unusual occurrences, on the Daily Operator's Report.

15. Parking Enforcement Agents who are assigned to operate Department motor vehicles on patrol are expected to

    A. disregard the posted speed limits to save time
    B. remove their seat belts on short trips
    C. show courtesy to other drivers on the road
    D. take the right of way at all intersections

15.____

16. The driver of a Department motor vehicle should

   A. leave the windows open when parking the vehicle in a garage
   B. drive the vehicle at approximately 10 miles per hour in a parking field
   C. be alert for indication of low engine oil pressure and over-heated engine
   D. start a cold vehicle by racing the engine for 5 minutes

17. The reason that all defects on a Department vehicle that have been observed by its driver should be noted on a Monthly Vehicle Report Form 49 is:

   A. This action will foster better safety practices among other Agents
   B. The source of the defect may be located easily by a trained mechanic
   C. All the facts of an accident will be reported promptly
   D. The District Commander will not have to make road calls

18. If the driver of a Department vehicle is involved in an accident, an Accident Report should be made out. This Report should include a full description of how the accident happened.
   Which one of the following statements would PROPERLY belong in an Accident Report?

   A. "The accident occurred at the intersection of Broadway and 42nd Street."
   B. "The operator of the department vehicle replaced the windshield wiper."
   C. "The vehicle was checked for gas and water before the patrol began."
   D. "A bus passed two parked vehicles."

19. When a Department vehicle is disabled, whom should the operator notify? The

   A. Traffic Department garage   B. Assistant Bureau Chief
   C. Police Department   D. District Commander

20. The PROPER way for an operator of a Department vehicle to report unusual occurrences with respect to the operation of the vehicle is to

   A. follow the same procedures as for reporting a defect
   B. request the Regional Commander to assign another vehicle
   C. phone the Bureau Chief as soon as possible
   D. make a note of the circumstances on the Daily Operator's Report

---

KEY (CORRECT ANSWERS)

1.	A	11.	D
2.	D	12.	A
3.	B	13.	B
4.	D	14.	B
5.	D	15.	C
6.	A	16.	C
7.	A	17.	B
8.	B	18.	A
9.	C	19.	D
10.	B	20.	D

TEST 2

DIRECTIONS: Each question or incomplete statement is followed by several suggested answers or completions. Select the one that *BEST* answers the question or completes the statement. *PRINT THE LETTER OF THE CORRECT ANSWER IN THE SPACE AT THE RIGHT.*

Questions 1-5.

DIRECTIONS: Questions 1 through 5 are based on the following reading passage. When answering these questions, use *ONLY* the information in this passage.

Stopping, standing, and parking of motor vehicles is regulated by law to keep the public highways open for a smooth flow of traffic, and to keep stopped vehicles from blocking intersections, driveways, signs, fire hydrants, and other areas that must be kept clear. These established regulations apply in all situations, unless otherwise indicated by signs. Other local restrictions are posted in the areas to which they apply. Three examples of these other types of restrictions, which may apply singly or in combination with one another are:

NO STOPPING - This means that a driver may not stop a vehicle for any purpose except when necessary to avoid interference with other vehicles, or in compliance with directions of a police officer or signal.

NO STANDING - This means that a driver may stop a vehicle only temporarily to actually receive or discharge passengers.

NO PARKING - This means that a driver may stop a vehicle only temporarily to actually load or unload merchandise or passengers. When stopped, it is advisable to turn on warning flashers if equipped with them. However, one should never use a directional signal for this purpose, because it may confuse other drivers. Some NO PARKING signs prohibit parking between certain hours on certain days.

For example, the sign may read NO PARKING 8 A.M. to 11 A.M. MONDAY, WEDNESDAY, FRIDAY. These signs are usually utilized on streets where cleaning operations take place on alternate days

1. The parking regulation that applies to fire hydrants is an example of _____ regulations. 1._____
   A. local   B. established   C. posted   D. temporary

2. When stopped in a NO PARKING zone, it is *advisable* to 2._____
   A. turn on the right directional signal to indicate to other drivers that you will remain stopped
   B. turn on the left directional signal to indicate to other drivers that you may be leaving the curb after a period of time
   C. turn on the warning flashers if your car is equipped with them
   D. put the vehicle in reverse so that the backup lights will be on to warn approaching cars that you have temporarily stopped

3. You may stop a vehicle temporarily to discharge passengers in an area under the restriction of a 3._____
   A. NO STOPPING - NO STANDING zone
   B. NO STANDING - NO PARKING zone
   C. NO PARKING - NO STOPPING zone
   D. NO STOPPING - NO STANDING - NO PARKING zone

4. A sign reads "NO PARKING 8 A.M. to 11 A.M., MONDAY, WEDNESDAY, FRIDAY." Based on this sign, a parking enforcement agent would issue a summons to a car that is parked on a

   A. Tuesday at 9:30 a.m.
   B. Wednesday at 12:00 a.m.
   C. Friday at 10:30 a.m.
   D. Saturday at 8:00 a.m.

5. NO PARKING signs prohibiting parking between certain hours, on certain days, are usually utilized on streets where

   A. vehicles frequently take on and discharge passengers
   B. cleaning operations take place on alternate days
   C. NO STOPPING signs have been ignored
   D. commercial vehicles take on and unload merchandise

Questions 6-15.

DIRECTIONS: Questions 6 through 15 are based on the following reading passage. When answering these questions, use ONLY the information in this passage.

Parking Enforcement Agents in Iron City work three shifts. The first shift is from 10 a.m. to 6 p.m. The second shift is from 6 p.m. to 2 a.m. The third shift is from 2 a.m. to 10 a.m. Each shift at the Central Office employs three people who patrol the surrounding area. Parking Enforcement Agents have one hour off per shift for lunch.

Starting on Tuesday, Agents Fred Black, Mary Evans, and Thomas Hart worked the first shift. Harold Wilson and Mary Wood worked the second shift. The third agent for the second shift was ill. Thomas Hart worked the second shift in addition to his regular first shift, and thus earned overtime pay. Mike Brown, Anne Hill, and Jeff Smith worked the third shift.

On his first shift, Agent Thomas Hart wrote 11 summonses for meter violations, 15 summonses for double parking, and 13 summonses for parking in a no-standing zone. On his second shift, Thomas Hart wrote 21 summonses for double parking, 13 summonses for meter violations, and 15 summonses for parking in a no-standing zone.

6. On Tuesday, Agent Mary Wood was on duty from

   A. 6 a.m. to 2 p.m.
   B. 10 a.m. to 6 p.m.
   C. 2 a.m. to 6 p.m.
   D. 6 p.m. to 2 a.m.

7. How many Parking Enforcement Agents normally work from 6 p.m. to 2 a.m.?

   A. One   B. Two   C. Three   D. Four

8. The number of Parking Enforcement Agents who *actually* worked the second shift on Tuesday was

   A. one   B. two   C. three   D. four

9. Among the three successive shifts which started on Tuesday, the total number of DIFFERENT Parking Enforcement Agents who *actually* reported for duty was

   A. 7   B. 8   C. 9   D. 10

10. The total number of summonses Agent Hart wrote during the FIRST shift he worked was

    A. 11   B. 13   C. 39   D. 49

11. Agent Hill was scheduled to finish her shift at 11.____

    A. 10 a.m.   B. 6 p.m.   C. 10 p.m.   D. 2 a.m.

12. Parking Enforcement Agents have one hour off per shift. The total hours *actually* worked 12.____
    by Agent Evans on Tuesday was

    A. 8 hours   B. 7 1/2 hours   C. 7 hours   D. 6 1/2 hours

13. The total number of summonses Agent Hart wrote for meter violations was 13.____

    A. 15   B. 24   C. 26   D. 34

14. During both his shifts, Agent Hart wrote the *MOST* summonses for 14.____

    A. A meter violations
    C. double parking
    B. standing in a no-parking zone
    D. parking in a no-standing zone

15. The total number of summonses Agent Hart wrote during his two shifts was 15.____

    A. 28   B. 48   C. 68   D. 88

Questions 16-20.

DIRECTIONS: Answer Questions 16 through 20 *ONLY* on the basis of the information contained in the street map and the accompanying explanatory information given below.

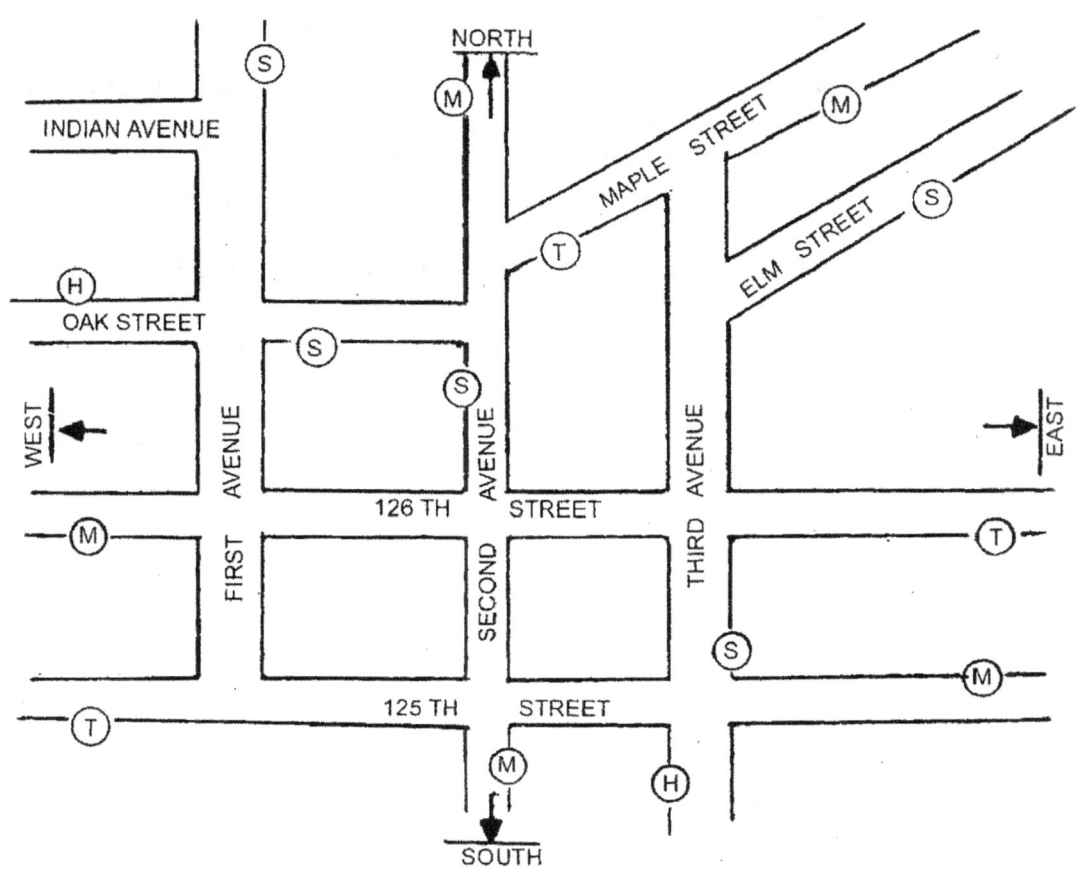

The map displayed above represents Parking Enforcement Agent Johnson's assigned area. The circled letters represent locations of special interest to him. Ⓜ is a meter location, Ⓗ is a fire hydrant location; Ⓢ is a bus stop; Ⓣ and is a taxi stand. Summonses are issued for parking at any of these locations.

16. Johnson was walking west on 126th Street. He made a left turn into 3rd Avenue. He issued a summons to a car parked on the east side of the street.
    For what type of violation did he issue this summons?

    A. Meter violation
    B. Parked at a fire hydrant
    C. Parked at a taxi stand
    D. Parked at a bus stop

17. Johnson was walking south on 1st Avenue. He made a right turn Into Oak Street. He issued a summons to a car parked on the north side of the street.
    For what type of violation did he issue this summons?

    A. Meter violation
    B. Parked at a fire hydrant
    C. Parked at a taxi stand
    D. Parked at a bus stop

18. Johnson was walking east on 125th Street. He made a left turn into 3rd Avenue and, at the first intersection, turned right into another street. He then issued a summons to the car parked on the south side of the street.
    For what type of violation did he issue this summons?

    A. Meter violation
    B. Parked at a fire hydrant
    C. Parked at a taxi stand
    D. Parked at a bus stop

19. Johnson was walking in a westerly direction on Maple Street. He made a left turn into 2nd Avenue and then made a left turn into 126th Street.
    In what direction would Jones be walking on 126th Street?

    A. East
    B. North
    C. West
    D. South

20. As shown on the map, with only the locations indicated, how many DIFFERENT types of violations could Johnson issue summonses for on 2nd Avenue?

    A. 1
    B. 2
    C. 3
    D. 4

KEY (CORRECT ANSWERS)

1. B
2. C
3. B
4. C
5. B

6. D
7. C
8. C
9. B
10. C

11. A
12. C
13. B
14. C
15. D

16. D
17. B
18. C
19. A
20. B

EXAMINATION SECTION
TEST 1

DIRECTIONS: Each question or incomplete statement is followed by several suggested answers or completions. Select the one that *BEST* answers the question or completes the statement. *PRINT THE LETTER OF THE CORRECT ANSWER IN THE SPACE AT THE RIGHT.*

Questions 1-5.

DIRECTIONS: Questions 1 through 5, inclusive, consist of groups of four displays representing license identification plates. Examine each group of plates and determine the number of plates in each group which are identical. Mark your answer sheets as follows:

If only two plates are identical, mark answer A.
If only three plates are identical, mark answer B.
If all four plates are identical, mark answer C.
If the plates are all different, mark answer D.

EXAMPLE

| ABC123 | BCD123 | ABC123 | BCD235 |

Since only two plates are identical, the first and the third, the correct answer is A.

1. | PBV839 | PVB839 | PVB839 | PVB839 |

2. | WTX083 | WTX083 | WTX083 | WTX083 |

3. | B73609 | D73906 | BD7396 | BD7906 |

4. | AK7423 | AK7423 | AK1423 | A81324 |

5. | 583Y10 | 683Y10 | 583Y01 | 583Y10 |

Questions 6-10.

DIRECTIONS: Questions 6 through 10 consist of groups of numbers and letters similar to those which might appear on license plates. Each group of numbers and letters will be called a license identification. Choose the license identification lettered A, B, C, or D that *EXACTLY* matches the license identifcation shown next to the question number.

2 (#1)

SAMPLE

NY 1977
ABC - 123

A. NY 1976 ABC - 123
B. NY 1977 ABC - 132
C. NY 1977 CBA - 123
D. NY 1977 ABC - 123

The license identification given is NY 1977 ABC-123. The only choice that exactly matches it is the license identification next to the letter D. The correct answer is therefore D.

6. NY 1976 QLT 781

    A. NJ 1976 QLT 781
    B. NY 1975 QLT 781
    C. NY 1976 QLT 781
    D. NY 1977 QLT 781

    6.____

7. FLA 1977 2-7LT58J

    A. FLA 1977 2-7TL58J
    B. FLA 1977 2-7LTJ58
    C. FLA 1977 2-7LT58J
    D. LA 1977 2-7LT58J

    7.____

8. NY 1975 OQC383

    A. NY 1975 OQC383
    B. NY 1975 OQC883
    C. NY 1975 OCQ383
    D. NY 1977 OCQ383

    8.____

9. MASS 1977 B-8DK02

    A. MISS 1977 B-8DK02
    B. MASS 1977 B-8DK02
    C. MASS 1976 B-8DK02
    D. MASS 1977 B-80KD2

    9.____

10. NY 1976 ZV0586

    A. NY 1976 2V0586
    B. NY 1977 ZV0586
    C. NY 1976 ZV0586
    D. NY 1976 ZU0586

    10.____

Questions 11-15.

DIRECTIONS: In copying the addresses below from Column A to the same line in Column B, an Agent-in-Training made some errors. For each question numbered 11 to 15, if you find that the Agent made an error in

only *one* line, mark your answer A
only *two* lines, mark your answer B
only *three* lines, mark your answer C
all *four* lines, mark your answer D

EXAMPLE

Column A	Column B
24 Third Avenue	24 Third Avenue
5 Lincoln Road	5 Lincoln Street
50 Central Park West	6 Central Park West
37-21 Queens Boulevard	21-37 Queens Boulevard

Since errors were made on only three lines, namely the second, third, and fourth, the correct answer is C.

Column A	Column B
11. 57-22 Springfield Boulevard	75-22 Springfield Boulevard
94 Gun Hill Road	94 Gun Hill Avenue
8 New Dorp Lane	8 New Drop Lane
36 Bedford Avenue	36 Bedford Avenue
12. 538 Castle Hill Avenue	538 Castle Hill Avenue
54-15 Beach Channel Drive	54-15 Beach Channel Drive
21 Ralph Avenue	21 Ralph Avenue
162 Madison Avenue	162 Morrison Avenue
13. 49 Thomas Street	49 Thomas Street
27-21 Northern Blvd.	21-27 Northern Blvd.
86 125th Street	86 125th Street
872 Atlantic Ave.	872 Baltic Ave.
14. 261-17 Horace Harding Expressway	261-17 Horace Harding Parkway
191 Fordham Road	191 Fordham Road
6 Victory Blvd.	6 Victoria Blvd.
552 Oceanic Ave.	552 Ocean Ave.
15. 90-05 38th Avenue	90-05 36th Avenue
19 Central Park West	19 Central Park East
9281 Avenue X	9281 Avenue X
22 West Farms Square	22 West Farms Square

11._____
12._____
13._____
14._____
15._____

16. A parking enforcement agent must become a special patrolman in order to issue summonses. A summons is a written legal order, in the name of The People of the State, signed by a special patrolman, which requires the person to whom addressed to appear and answer the patrolman's charge at a specified time, date, and place.
According to the paragraph above, the reason that a parking enforcement agent is required to become a special patrolman is that a special patrolman is authorized to

    A. carry a loaded weapon
    B. answer specified charges from The People of the State
    C. serve a summons in the city
    D. adopt new parking regulations for the city

17. All summonses and stubs which have been issued to a parking enforcement agent must be accounted for by that agent. The agent must report to the district commander, without delay, any such summons or copy that has been damaged, lost, or stolen, or contains errors. Members of the force are not permitted to make changes or corrections on a summons or copy.
According to the paragraph above, the rule about correcting errors on a summons is that the

    A. district commander makes all changes on the summons
    B. parking enforcement agent makes changes on a copy of the summons
    C. parking enforcement agent makes changes on a damaged copy of the summons only
    D. summons must not be changed in any way

18. A procedure of the traffic control bureau concerned with the issuance of a summons for overtime parking in a metered space states:
    A summons shall be served by placing it under the windshield wiper.
Which one of the following possible reasons for this procedure is the *MOST* logical?

    A. Passing motorists will be made aware of the parking restrictions.
    B. The driver will see it and then put a coin into the meter.
    C. A passing police officer will see it and issue another summons.
    D. The summons is less likely to be lost before the driver returns.

19. If you find that there are not enough blank lines on a standard departmental report form to include all of the information you want to write in, how should you complete your report?

    A. Put this form aside and write your report on a blank paper
    B. Leave out some details called for on the report which seem unimportant
    C. Double the number of written lines by reducing your lettering to half-size
    D. Attach another sheet with the additional information written on it

20. Summonses must be served in numerical order. Which one of the following sequences of nine-digit numbers is in the correct numerical order?

    A. 69 088175-9; 69 088175-8; 69 088175-5; 69 088175-6
    B. 69 316958-4; 69 316958-5; 69 316958-6; 69 316958-7
    C. 68 088176-1; 68 088176-3; 68 088176-5; 68 088176-2
    D. 68 316950-5; 68 316950-2; 68 316950-3; 68 316950-4

KEY (CORRECT ANSWERS)

1. B
2. C
3. D
4. A
5. A

6. C
7. C
8. A
9. B
10. C

11. C
12. A
13. B
14. C
15. B

16. C
17. D
18. D
19. D
20. B

TEST 2

DIRECTIONS: Each question or incomplete statement is followed by several suggested answers or completions. Select the one that *BEST* answers the question or completes the statement. *PRINT THE LETTER OF THE CORRECT ANSWER IN THE SPACE AT THE RIGHT.*

Questions 1-20.

DIRECTIONS: Each of Questions 1 through 20 consists of a sentence in which a word is italicized. Of the four words following each sentence, choose the word whose meaning is *most nearly* the *SAME* as the meaning of the italicized word.

1. The Agent's first *assignment* was to patrol on Hicks Avenue. 1.____
   A. test B. sign C. job D. deadline

2. Agents get many *inquiries* from the public. 2.____
   A. complaints B. suggestions
   C. compliments D. questions

3. The names of all fifty states were written in *abbreviated* form. 3.____
   A. shortened B. corrected C. eliminated D. illegible

4. The meter was examined and found to be *defective*. 4.____
   A. small B. operating C. destroyed D. faulty

5. Agent Roger's reports are *legible*, but Agent Baldwin's are not. 5.____
   A. similar B. readable C. incorrect D. late

6. The time allowed, as shown by the meter, had *expired*. 6.____
   A. started B. broken C. ended D. violated

7. The busy *commercial* area is quiet in the evenings. 7.____
   A. deserted B. growing C. business D. local

8. The district office *authorized* the giving of summonses to illegally parked trucks. 8.____
   A. suggested B. approved C. prohibited D. recorded

9. Department property must be used *exclusively* for official business. 9.____
   A. occasionally B. frequently C. only D. properly

10. The District Commander *banned* driving in the area. 10.____
    A. detoured B. permitted C. encouraged D. prohibited

11. Two copies of the summons are *retained* by the Parking Enforcement Agent. 11.____
    A. kept B. distributed C. submitted D. signed

12. The Agent *detected* a parking violation. 12.____

    A. cancelled   B. discovered   C. investigated   D. reported

13. *Pedestrians* may be given summonses for violating traffic regulations. 13.____

    A. bicycle riders   B. horsemen
    C. motorcyclists   D. walkers

14. Parked cars are not allowed to *obstruct* traffic. 14.____

    A. direct   B. lead   C. block   D. speed

15. It was *obvious* to the Agent that the traffic light was broken. 15.____

    A. uncertain   B. surprising   C. possible   D. clear

16. The signs stated that parking in the area was *restricted* to vehicles of foreign diplomats. 16.____

    A. allowed   B. increased   C. desired   D. limited

17. Each parking violation carries an *appropriate* fine. 17.____

    A. suitable   B. extra   C. light   D. heavy

18. Strict enforcement of parking regulations helps to *alleviate* traffic congestion. 18.____

    A. extend   B. build   C. relieve   D. increase

19. The Traffic Control Bureau has a rule which states that an Agent shall speak and act *courteously* in any relationship with the public. 19.____

    A. respectfully   B. timidly
    C. strangely   D. intelligently

20. City traffic regulations prohibit parking at *jammed* meters. 20.____

    A. stuck   B. timed   C. open   D. installed

KEY (CORRECT ANSWERS)

1.	C	11.	A
2.	D	12.	B
3.	A	13.	D
4.	D	14.	C
5.	B	15.	D
6.	C	16.	D
7.	C	17.	A
8.	B	18.	C
9.	C	19.	A
10.	D	20.	A

EXAMINATION SECTION
TEST 1

DIRECTIONS: Each question or incomplete statement is followed by several suggested answers or completions. Select the one that BEST answers the question or completes the statement. *PRINT THE LETTER OF THE CORRECT ANSWER IN THE SPACE AT THE RIGHT.*

1. One of the main functions of the Parking Meter Division of the Department of Finance is to *collect and account for revenue deposited in parking meters and to cooperate with the Department of Traffic and its contractors to install and maintain parking meters in efficient and maximum revenue-producing operation.*
   According to this statement, it is reasonable to assume that employees of the Parking Meter Division are NOT expected to

   A. report to their supervisor the number of parking meters which are not working
   B. place traffic summonses on cars illegally parked at meters so as to increase parking revenue collections
   C. cooperate with contractors installing new parking meters
   D. keep accurate and up-to-date records of coin boxes taken from parking meters, both in parking lots and street curb locations

   1.____

2. A parking meter collector should not allow any coin container to be out of his possession until he delivers it to the departmental vehicle.
   Of the following, the BEST reason for this rule is that

   A. the containers are heavy and only a physically strong person can carry this load of coins
   B. too much time would be lost if coin containers are handled more than once
   C. responsibility for the container is fixed, and loss is prevented
   D. the public expects each city employee to do his own job without help from anyone else

   2.____

3. An IMPORTANT result of the use of parking meters in busy shopping and business areas is that there is

   A. less traffic delay because drivers are able to find parking space quickly and easily
   B. a fairer distribution of parking spaces in these areas of the city
   C. a greater opportunity to keep the streets clean by eliminating the all-day parkers
   D. a stricter enforcement of traffic regulations by the Police Department to keep traffic flowing smoothly

   3.____

4. All men appointed as parking meter collectors must be bonded.
   The PRINCIPAL reason for this requirement is to

   A. act as a further check on the parking meter collector's character
   B. make sure that the parking meter collector is competent to do his work
   C. insure that job applicants are seriously interested in the job
   D. protect the city against financial loss

   4.____

5. While you are making collections as a parking meter collector on a side street, you observe attached to three parking meters cardboard signs on which is hand-printed *No Parking Today - Police Department*. You know that these signs were put up by unauthorized individuals.
You should

   A. let the signs remain; someone else will probably remove them within a short time
   B. remove the signs; save them and use them yourself when official circumstances require it
   C. let the signs remain; someone must have had a good reason to put them there
   D. remove the signs; they were not put there by authorized police officers

6. While you are at work as a parking meter collector, the driver of a private car parks his car near you at a metered space. This driver asks you to watch his car and its valuable contents *for only five minutes* while he does an errand.
You should

   A. politely inform the driver of the private car that you are unable to help him
   B. assure the driver of the private car that his car and its contents will be safe
   C. tell the driver of the private car you can watch his car only for as long as you are actually in the area
   D. watch the private car for the five minutes and thus create goodwill for the city

7. While you are driving the collection truck to collect the meter money on Z Street, it becomes obvious that Z Street is closed and barricaded due to a very serious water main break and undermining of the roadway.
It would be BEST to

   A. go in on foot and make the collection
   B. postpone the collection to a later date
   C. remove the barricade and carefully drive into the street to collect the meter money
   D. wait a few hours until the water goes down

8. You are collecting coin boxes from parking meters and placing them in a small cart which is about half-filled with boxes containing money. You are about fifty feet from the corner where a fire alarm box is located. Suddenly, a woman rushes from a house near you yelling *Fire*.
Of the following, the BEST action for you to take would be to

   A. go to the woman and ask her where the fire is
   B. have the woman sit on the stoop and try to calm her
   C. run to the fire alarm box and turn in an alarm
   D. direct the woman to the fire alarm box

9. As a parking meter collector, you frequently notice the same individual on the corner of X and Y Streets as you are making collections.
You should regard this man as

   A. an individual who is within his rights in being on the corner
   B. a person who is probably a meter vandal
   C. a person who should be asked by you what he is doing there
   D. an undercover law enforcement officer

10. As a parking meter collector, you have noticed that after repairs have been made in the shop, the coin door locks on the meters always require a major final adjustment in the field to be in really good working order.
    You should

    A. make no mention of it since the error will be discovered soon enough
    B. make this adjustment yourself if you can
    C. report this fact to your supervisor
    D. visit the repair shop and call it to the attention of the mechanics

11. An individual in your collection area volunteers the information to you, a parking meter collector, that he thinks the nearby ABC Hardware Store is a source of slugs that have been widely used in the local area in parking meters.
    You, as a parking meter collector, should

    A. regard this as probably the complaint of a disgruntled crank
    B. give this information to the proper authorities
    C. try to verify this information by further investigation yourself
    D. visit the ABC Hardware Store and tell the owner what you have heard

12. Of the following, the BEST reason for frequent collection of coin boxes from parking meters is that

    A. the city needs the money quickly
    B. overtime parkers can be discovered
    C. losses from meters that are broken into will be reduced
    D. the coin boxes are easier to handle when not full

Questions 13-14.

DIRECTIONS: Questions 13 and 14 are to be answered according to the information contained in the following paragraph.

The driver of the collection crew shall at all times remain in or on a department vehicle in which there is revenue. In the event such driver must leave the vehicle, he shall designate one of the other members of the crew to remain in or on the vehicle. The member of the crew so designated by the driver shall remain in or on the vehicle until relieved by the driver or another member of the crew. The vehicle may be left unattended only when there is no revenue contained therein provided, however, that in that event the vehicle shall be locked. The loss of any vehicle or any of its contents, including revenue, resulting from any deviation from this rule, shall be the responsibility of the member or members of crew who shall be guilty of such deviation.

13. The vehicle of a collection crew may be left with no one in it only if

    A. it is locked
    B. there is a crew member nearby
    C. there is no money in it
    D. there is only one member in the crew

14. If money is stolen from an unattended vehicle of a collection crew, the employee held responsible is the

    A. driver
    B. one who left the vehicle unattended
    C. one who left the vehicle unlocked
    D. one who relieved the driver

Questions 15-17.

DIRECTIONS: Questions 15 to 17 are to be answered according to the information given in the following paragraphs.

Off-Street Parking

The municipal parking system now consists of 23 off-street parking facilities: three garages and twenty parking fields. During 1986, four off-street parking areas were opened: a 420-space garage at Jerome Avenue-190th Street in the Bronx, an 88-space parking field at Jerome Avenue-170th Street also in the Bronx, a 59-space Sheepshead Bay parking field in Brooklyn, and a 39-space Leonard Street field in Manhattan. This brings to 8,000 the number of municipal off-street parking spaces now available.

On-street parking turnover was achieved at an additional 4.3 miles of unmetered curb space in shopping areas by the installation of signs limiting parking to one or two hours. An estimated two million short-term parkers are served annually in these spaces.

15. The number of off-street parking spaces available before the additions in 1986 was

    A. 7,639   B. 7,394   C. 7,606   D. 7,493

16. The LEAST correct statement is that the off-street parking facilities added to the municipal parking system in 1986 are MAINLY

    A. in the Bronx
    B. garages
    C. parking fields
    D. under 100 capacity

17. Increased on-street parking turnover at more than four miles of unmetered curb space in shopping areas was obtained by

    A. building garages
    B. opening parking fields
    C. putting in more parking meters
    D. putting in signs to limit parking

Questions 18-20.

DIRECTIONS: Answer Questions 18 to 20 according to the information contained in the following paragraph.

Each parking meter collector shall keep a permanently bound notebook record of each day's field activities, noting therein the date, area and the numbers of the meters from which collections were made or which were serviced by him. While at the meter, he shall also note therein any reason why a coin box was not collected or bulk revenue was not collected, the number and denominations of all loose coins found in the coin compartment of a coin box meter, those meters which are damaged in any respect and the nature of such damage, why a meter was not placed in operation, and any other information or circumstance which may affect the collections, revenue, operation, or maintenance of the meters he serviced. Any damage to collection equipment and the nature of the damage shall also be noted in such book. All such notations shall be set forth on the prescribed daily report form to be made out by the employee at the conclusion of each day's assignment. Said report shall be signed by all of the members of the collection crew.

18. The term *bulk revenue* in the above passage MOST probably refers to

    A. money not in a coin box
    B. money in a coin box
    C. money not taken from a meter
    D. paper money

19. A parking meter collector finds 60? in loose coins (three nickels, two dimes, one quarter) in the coin compartment of a coin box meter.
    Of the following, the BEST way to enter this in his notebook is *loose coins*

    A. 60¢
    B. 2 dimes, 3 nickels, 1 quarter
    C. 6, 60¢ total
    D. 3 Jefferson nickels, 2 Roosevelt dimes, 1 Washington quarter

20. The parking meter collector's daily report form is MAINLY 20. intended to be used to report the

    A. activities of collection crews with more than one or two members
    B. information not recorded in the bound notebook
    C. information recorded in the bound notebook
    D. unusual occurrences of the day

Questions 21-25.

DIRECTIONS: Answer Questions 21 to 25 only according to the information given in the following chart.

COLLECTION DIVISION
PARKING METER FIELD
OPERATION REPORT

Date : Jan . 4 ,

Location	Time Arrived	Time Departed	Elapsed Time Travel Hr. Min.		Collection Hr. Min.	
Office		9:15				
2407	10:00	10:35		45		35
3502	10:45	11:15		10		30
2574	11:20	12:50		5	1	30
Lunch	1:05	2:05		15		
3379	2:05	2:55				50
2810	3:05	3:30		10		25
3208	3:35	4:00		5		25
Office	4:45			45		

Total _____   _____

Remarks : _____

Vehicle No. _____

Mileage: Start 174

Total Crew _____

Close 209

Daily Total   35   Parking Meter Areas Assigned: 2407, 3502,
2574, 3379,
2810, 3208

James Roe
Driver

21. According to the information in the report, and assuming equal traffic conditions, which of the following statements about the distances between locations is TRUE?   21.___

   A. If the crew car was always driven at an average speed of 25 miles an hour, the crew never travelled less than 2 miles to get from one location to another.
   B. The last location the crew worked at was farther from the office than the first location they worked at.
   C. The place where the crew ate lunch was right near the last place they worked at before lunch.
   D. Travelling from one assigned parking meter area to the next, the crew never travelled as far as when they went from the first to the second location they worked at.

22. Which of the following items of information can be gotten from the report?   22.___

   A. Average time spent collecting at each location
   B. The license of the vehicle
   C. When the crew got to the office in the morning
   D. When the crew left the office in the afternoon

23. Suppose that, on the average, the same amount of time was spent by a parking meter collector in collecting from any meter.
Therefore, according to the report, the parking meter area that had approximately one-third as many meters as the area 2574 is

   A. 2407 B. 3502 C. 3379 D. 2810

24. Information which CANNOT be gotten from this report alone is the

   A. distance travelled
   B. total time spent collecting
   C. number of meters collected from
   D. total time spent travelling

25. Judging from the information in the report, it is MOST probable that

   A. members of the crew took turns driving
   B. nothing unusual happened to this crew that day
   C. the crew did not take their full time for lunch
   D. the crew was made up of a driver and a collector

KEY (CORRECT ANSWERS)

1.	B		11.	B
2.	C		12.	C
3.	B		13.	C
4.	D		14.	B
5.	D		15.	B
6.	A		16.	B
7.	B		17.	D
8.	D		18.	A
9.	A		19.	B
10.	C		20.	C

21.	A
22.	A
23.	B
24.	C
25.	B

EXAMINATION SECTION
TEST 1

DIRECTIONS: Each question or incomplete statement is followed by several suggested answers or completions. Select the one that BEST answers the question or completes the statement. *PRINT THE LETTER OF THE CORRECT ANSWER IN THE SPACE AT THE RIGHT.*

1. A parking meter collector, taking out the sealed coin boxes from the parking meters on one block, notices that the box from one of the meters weighs much less than the other boxes.
   Unless there are other indications, the collector should suspect that

   A. by the law of averages, this box will probably be the heaviest next time
   B. the block is not good for parking
   C. this box is made of a newer and lighter metal
   D. this meter is not in good order

   1.____

2. A parking meter collector on his way home from work sees two men trying to pry open a parking meter.
   Of the following, the BEST action for the collector to take is to

   A. advise the men to stop, explaining the unlawful aspects of such action
   B. call a policeman and point out the men and the meter
   C. ignore the incident as it is a matter for the police
   D. watch the men but do nothing unless they actually break the meter

   2.____

3. A parking meter collector at work notices that the time has expired on a parking meter in front of which a car is parked.
   He should

   A. continue with his work and pay no attention to this matter
   B. copy down the license number of the car and forward it to the Police Department
   C. find the owner of the car and tell him to deposit a dime in the meter
   D. report the matter to his superior

   3.____

4. A parking meter collector is asked for street directions by a passerby.
   The collector should

   A. give the directions if he knows them
   B. politely inform the passerby that if he answered every request for directions he wouldn't have time to do his work
   C. suspect a possible hold-up
   D. tell the passerby to go find a policeman

   4.____

5. A collector opening a meter to remove the coin box finds, in addition to the coin box, some loose dimes in the meter housing.
   He should

   A. remove the coin box and leave the dimes, calling attention to them in his report
   B. remove the coin box and put the dimes into the nearby meters
   C. take the meter out of service by putting a hood over it and leave the coin box and loose money
   D. turn in the coin box and the dimes to the office and include an explanation in his report

   5.____

6. A parking meter collector who had reason to believe that someone had been trying to open the parking meters in a particular block reported the situation to his superior. The action of the collector was

   A. *unwise* since he should have kept the area under observation for a longer time and waited until he had more facts before he reported to his superior
   B. *wise* since in this way he shifted the responsibility to the higher-ups
   C. *unwise* since if he had informed the Police Department, quicker action would have resulted
   D. *wise* since the superior will be able to see to it that appropriate action is taken

7. A collector finds that a parking meter and the parking space beside it have been completely surrounded by scaffolding for a repair job so that he is unable to get to the meter to remove the coin box.
   The BEST way to describe this situation on the collector's report would be:

   A. Coin box may not be removed
   B. Meter not working
   C. Meter cannot be reached because of construction
   D. No revenue

8. Suppose that a hood is placed over a parking meter when it is out of order and removed after the meter has been repaired. A collector, in his instructions for the day, is told to remove the hood from Meter 97 and put in a coin box. After doing this, he finds that he cannot lock the meter.
   The collector should

   A. follow out his instructions by removing the hood and putting in a coin box and report that he could not lock the meter
   B. leave everything as he found it and report the meter for repair
   C. leave the coin box in but put the hood back
   D. leave the hood off but take out the coin box and submit a report

9. Suppose that while you are at work, a citizen asks you how much money the city collects from parking meters. The BEST action for you to take is to

   A. ask him why he wants these figures
   B. inform him that such information is never given orally
   C. refer him to the office of your department
   D. tell him that in your opinion this matter is of no concern of his

10. A key breaks off in the lock while the collector is closing the meter.
    MOST probably, this happened because the

    A. key was too new
    B. key was weak and defective
    C. lock was closed too fast
    D. meter was not completely broken in

11. Suppose that to open a meter a collector must pick, from a ring with many keys, the key with the same serial number as the meter.
    If a parking meter collector is having difficulty getting the key he has picked from the ring into the lock of a meter, he should FIRST

    A. check the number of the key and meter
    B. put some lead or graphite into the lock
    C. rub some lead or graphite on the key
    D. use pressure to force the key into the lock

12. While a collector is opening a parking meter, a small boy snatches one of the loaded coin boxes from the collector's push truck that is on the sidewalk and runs away.
    The BEST action for the collector to take would be to

    A. call out *Stop, thief!* in a loud voice and attract the attention of the driver of the Parking Meter Division truck nearby
    B. check his records quickly to see if the snatched coin box was empty or full
    C. fix in his mind a good description of the boy to give to the police later because it is no use trying to have the boy caught
    D. quickly close the parking meter and then run after the boy right away to try and catch him

13. While a collector was at work collecting coin boxes from meters, a group of curious onlookers crowded around him to watch him work. The collector asked the people to move back.
    The action of the collector in this case was

    A. *foolish* because it will only serve to antagonize the public
    B. *sensible* because a crowd can sometimes end up in a riot
    C. *foolish* because the people will not be able to see the operations clearly from further back
    D. *sensible* because the collector will not be interfered with in his work

14. Of the following, the MAIN reason for using parking meters is that it

    A. clears congested areas of all parked cars and permits easier cleaning of the streets
    B. ends double parking and cruising in search of parking space
    C. eliminates the all-day parker and makes more curb space available for short-time parkers
    D. greatly increases the revenue

15. A parking meter collector should report to his superior any broken pavements in parking meter areas MAINLY because

    A. a collector should inform his superior of everything that happens on his route
    B. broken pavements may prevent motorists from using the parking meter area and result in loss of revenue
    C. the break may be due to a burst water main
    D. the Parking Meter Division is required to fix all broken street areas

16. A parking meter collector must work outdoors under all sorts of weather conditions. This is an important reason for requiring an applicant for this job to be

    A. in good physical condition
    B. thoroughly familiar with the geography of the city
    C. well-dressed at all times
    D. willing to work at any hour of the day or night

17. A parking meter collector should submit full and complete reports about defective meters.
Of the following, the BEST reason for requiring complete reports is that

    A. a long report is usually better than a short one because it gives more information
    B. it gives the collector good experience in the writing of proper reports
    C. reports are usually kept as permanent records
    D. the maintenance crew will be better able to plan repairs

18. When a parking meter collector must be absent because of illness, he should notify his superior as soon as possible. Of the following, the BEST reason for this rule is that it

    A. gives the department a chance to send medical assistanc to the collector
    B. makes it possible for the department to keep a check on the health of its employees
    C. provides a definite record for the timekeeper which cannot later be denied by the employee
    D. provides notice to the supervisor so that he can cover any essential work which must be performed

19. An employee must report all injuries received on the job. Of the following, the BEST reason for this rule is that it

    A. helps to prevent the occurrence of similar accidents
    B. makes the employee get medical attention
    C. prevents unnecessary lawsuits against the city
    D. provides a means of accumulating accident statistics

20. Employees should consult the official bulletin board regularly. Of the following, the BEST reason for this rule is that

    A. an employee's interest in his work is developed in this way
    B. employees are given a place where they can contact each other
    C. employees are kept informed of all social activities in the department
    D. new orders and procedures are posted on the bulletin board

21. The areas finally selected for the installation of parking meters are carefully chosen after long-range studies have been made to determine the frequency of use of the area for parking purposes by operators of vehicles. According to this statement, it is MOST reasonable to assume that

    A. one purpose of the studies is to find out the popularit of different neighborhoods
    B. parking meters are installed in only a small portion of the areas studied
    C. parking meters are not put in neighborhoods which have not been studied
    D. the studies made take a few days

22. It has been proved that an employee who is interested in his job is more efficient than another employee with equal ability who is not interested in his job.
According to this statement, it is MOST probable that

    A. all employees who are efficient are interested in their jobs
    B. employees are more or less equal in ability, and differences in efficiency are due to differences in interest
    C. employees who are not efficient are not interested in their jobs
    D. some employees who are producing more and better work than before may have developed an interest in their jobs

23. An inexperienced or untrained observe overlooks important details and fails to distinguish the comparative importance of those that he sees.
According to this statement,

    A. an experienced observer overlooks no detail, no matter how minor
    B. an inexperienced observer cannot see to what degree one detail is more important than another
    C. an untrained observer sees the unimportant details but not the important ones
    D. a trained observer pays no attention to unimportant details

Questions 24-27.

DIRECTIONS.   Questions 24 to 27 must be answered according to the information given in the paragraph below.

It is an accepted fact that the rank and file employee can frequently advance worthwhile suggestions toward increasing efficiency. For this reason, an Employees' Suggestion System has been developed and put into operation. Suitable means have been provided at each departmental location for the confidential submission of suggestions. Numerous suggestions have been received thus far and., after study, about five percent of the ideas submitted are being translated into action. It is planned to set up, eventually, monetary awards for all worthwhile suggestions.

24. According to the paragraph above, a MAJOR reason why an Employees' Suggestion System was established is that

    A. an organized program of improvement is better than a haphazard one
    B. employees can often given good suggestions to increase efficiency
    C. once a fact is accepted, it is better to act on it than to do nothing
    D. the suggestions of rank and file employees were being neglected

25. According to the paragraph above, under the Employees' Suggestion System,

    A. a file of worthwhile suggestions will eventually be set up at each departmental location
    B. it is possible for employees to turn in suggestions without fellow employees knowing of it
    C. means have been provided for the regular and frequent collection of suggestions submitted
    D. provision has been made for the judging of worthwhile suggestions by an Employees' Suggestion Committee

26. According to the paragraph above, it is reasonable to assume that

    A. all suggestions must be turned in at a central office
    B. employees who make worthwhile suggestions will be promoted
    C. not all the prizes offered will be monetary ones
    D. prizes of money will be given for the best suggestions

27. According to the paragraph above, of the many suggestions made,

    A. all are first tested
    B. a small part are put into use
    C. most are very worthwhile
    D. samples are studied

Questions 28-31.

DIRECTIONS: Questions 28 to 31 must be answered according to the information given in the paragraph below.

Employees may be granted leaves of absence without pay at the discretion of the Personnel Officer. Such a leave without pay shall begin on the first working day on which the employee does not report for duty and shall continue to the first day on which the employee returns to duty. The Personnel Division may vary the dates of the leave for the record so as to conform with payroll periods, but in no case shall an employee be off the payroll for a different number of calendar days than would have been the case if the actual dates mentioned above had been used. An employee who has vacation or overtime to his credit, which is available for normal use, may take time off immediately prior to beginning a leave of absence without pay, chargeable against all or part of such vacation or overtime.

28. According to the paragraph above, the Personnel Officer must

    A. decide if a leave of absence without pay should be granted
    B. require that a leave end on the last working day of a payroll period
    C. see to it that a leave of absence begins on the first working day of a pay period
    D. vary the dates of a leave of absence to conform with a payroll period

29. According to the paragraph above, the exact dates of a leave of absence without pay may be varied provided that the

    A. calendar days an employee is off the payroll equal the actual leave granted
    B. leave conforms to an even number of payroll periods
    C. leave when granted made provision for variance to simplify payroll records
    D. Personnel Officer approves the variation

30. According to the paragraph above, a leave of absence without pay must extend from the

    A. first day of a calendar period to the first day the employee resumes work
    B. first day of a payroll period to the last calendar day of the leave
    C. first working day missed to the first day on which the employee resumes work
    D. last day on which an employee works through the first day he returns to work

31. According to the paragraph above, an employee may take extra time off just before the start of a leave of absence without pay if   31._____

    A. he charges this extra time against his leave
    B. he has a favorable balance of vacation or overtime which has been frozen
    C. the vacation or overtime that he would normally use for a leave without pay has not been charged in this way before
    D. there is time to his credit which he may use

Questions 32-34.

DIRECTIONS: Questions 32 to 34 must be answered according to the information given in the paragraph below.

The regulations applying to parking meters provide that the driver is required to deposit the appropriate coin immediately upon parking, and it is illegal for him to return at a later period to extend the parking time. If there is unused time on a parking meter, another oar may be parked for a period not to exceed the unused time without the deposit of a coin. Operators of commercial vehicles are not required to deposit coins while loading or unloading expeditiously. By definition, a vehicle is considered parked even though there is a driver at the wheel and the meter must be used by the driver of such car.

32. According to the paragraph above, the regulations applying to parking meters do NOT   32._____

    A. allow the driver of a parked vehicle to stay in his car
    B. consider any loading or unloading of a vehicle as parking
    C. make any distinction between an unoccupied car and one with the driver at the wheel
    D. permit a driver who has parked a car at a meter with unused parking time to put a coin in the meter

33. According to the paragraph above, it is a violation of the parking meter regulations to   33._____

    A. load and unload slowly
    B. park commercial vehicles except for loading and unloading
    C. put a second coin in the meter in order to park longer
    D. use a parking space at any time without depositing a coin

34. The paragraph above clearly indicates   34._____

    A. the number of minutes a vehicle may be parked
    B. the value of the coin that is to be put in the meter
    C. what is meant by a commercial vehicle
    D. when a car may be parked free

Questions 35-40.

DIRECTIONS: Questions 35 to 40 must be answered according to the information given in the paragraph below.

There are many types of reports. One of these is the field report, which requests information specified and grouped under columns or headings. A detailed, printed form is often used in submitting field reports. However, these printed, standardized forms provide a limited amount of space. The field man is required to make the decision as to how much of the information he has should go directly into the report and how much should be left for clarification if and when he is called in to explain a reported finding. In many instances, the addition of a short explanation of the finding might relieve the reader of the report of the necessity to seek an explanation. Therefore, the basic factual information asked for by the printed report form should often be clarified by some simple explanatory statement. If this is done, the reported finding becomes meaningful to the reader of the report who is far from the scene of the subject matter dealt with in the report. The significance of that which is reported finds its expression in the adoption of certain policies, improvements, or additions essential to furthering the effectiveness of the program.

35. According to the paragraph above, the field report asks for

   A. a detailed statement of the facts
   B. field information which comes under the heading of technical data
   C. replies to well-planned questions
   D. specific information in different columns

36. According to the paragraph above, the usual printed field report form

   A. does not have much room for writing
   B. is carefully laid out
   C. is necessary for the collection of facts
   D. usually has from three to four columns

37. According to the paragraph above, the man in the field must decide if

   A. a report is needed at all
   B. he should be called in to explain a reported finding
   C. he should put all the information he has into the report
   D. the reader of the report is justified in seeking an explanation

38. According to the paragraph above, the man in the field may be required to

   A. be acquainted with the person or persons who will read his report
   B. explain the information he reports
   C. give advice on specific problems
   D. keep records of the amount of work he completes

39. According to the paragraph above, the value of an explanatory statement added to the factual information reported in the printed forms is that it

   A. allows the person making the report to express himself briefly
   B. forces the person making the report to think logically
   C. helps the report reader understand the facts reported
   D. makes it possible to turn in the report later

40. According to the paragraph above, the importance of the information given by the field man in his report is shown by the

    A. adoption of policies and improvements
    B. effectiveness of the field staff
    C. fact that such a report is required
    D. necessary cost studies to back up the facts

41. *The officer refuted the statement of the driver.*
As used in this sentence, the word *refuted* means MOST NEARLY

    A. disproved   B. elaborated upon
    C. related   D. supported

42. *The mechanism of the parking meter is not intricate.*
As used in this sentence, the word *intricate* means MOST NEARLY

    A. cheap   B. complicated   C. foolproof   D. strong

43. *The weight of each coin box fluctuates.*
As used in this sentence, the word *fluctuates* means MOST NEARLY

    A. always changes   B. decreases
    C. increases gradually   D. is similar

44. *The person chosen to investigate the new procedure should be impartial.*
As used in this sentence, the word *impartial* means MOST NEARLY

    A. experienced   B. fair
    C. forward looking   D. important

45. *A significant error was made by the collector.*
As used in this sentence, the word *significant* means MOST NEARLY

    A. doubtful   B. foolish   C. important   D. strange

46. *It is better to disperse a crowd.*
As used in this sentence, the word *disperse* means MOST NEARLY

    A. hold back   B. quiet   C. scatter   D. talk to

47. *Business groups wish to expand the parking meter program.*
As used in this sentence, the word *expand* means MOST NEARLY

    A. advertise   B. defeat   C. enlarge   D. expose

48. *The procedure was altered to assist the storekeepers.*
As used in this sentence, the word *altered* means MOST NEARLY

    A. abolished   B. changed
    C. improved   D. made simpler

49. *The collector was instructed to survey the damage to the parking meter.*
As used in this sentence, the word *survey* means MOST NEARLY

    A. examine   B. give the reason for
    C. repair   D. report

50. *It is imperative that a collector's report be turned in after each collection.*
    As used in this sentence, the word *imperative* means MOST NEARLY

    A. desired   B. recommended   C. requested   D. urgent

51. *The collector was not able to extricate the key.*
    As used in this sentence, the word *extricate* means MOST NEARLY

    A. find
    C. have a copy made of
    B. free
    D. turn

52. *Parking meters have alleviated one of our major traffic problems.*
    As used in this sentence, the word *alleviated* means MOST NEARLY

    A. created   B. lightened   C. removed   D. solved

53. *Formerly drivers with learners' permits could drive only on designated streets.*
    As used in this sentence, the word *designated* means MOST NEARLY

    A. dead-end   B. not busy   C. one way   D. specified

54. *Some traffic sign is required where a traffic hazard exists.*
    As used in this sentence, the word *hazard* means MOST NEARLY

    A. condition   B. danger   C. problem   D. stoppage

55. *Attempts have been made to impede the parking meter program.*
    As used in this sentence, the word *impede* means MOST NEARLY

    A. explain   B. ignore   C. obstruct   D. speed up

56. *Carelessness in the safekeeping of parking meter keys will not be tolerated.*
    As used in this sentence, the word *tolerated* means MOST NEARLY

    A. forgotten   B. permitted   C. punished lightly   D. understood

57. *The traffic was easily diverted.*
    As used in this sentence, the word *diverted* means MOST NEARLY

    A. controlled   B. speeded up   C. stopped   D. turned aside

58. *A transcript of the report was prepared in the office.*
    As used in this sentence, the word *transcript* means MOST NEARLY

    A. brief   B. copy   C. record   D. translation

59. *The change was authorized by the supervisor.*
    As used in this sentence, the word *authorized* means MOST NEARLY

    A. completed   B. corrected   C. ordered   D. permitted

60. *The supervisor read the excerpt of the collector's report.*
    According to this sentence, the supervisor read

    A. a passage from the report
    C. the original of the report
    B. a summary of the report
    D. the whole of the report

KEY (CORRECT ANSWERS)

1. D	11. A	21. C	31. D	41. A	51. B
2. B	12. A	22. D	32. C	42. B	52. B
3. A	13. D	23. B	33. C	43. A	53. D
4. A	14. C	24. B	34. D	44. B	54. B
5. D	15. B	25. B	35. D	45. C	55. C
6. D	16. A	26. D	36. A	46. C	56. B
7. C	17. D	27. B	37. C	47. C	57. D
8. B	18. D	28. A	38. B	48. B	58. B
9. C	19. A	29. A	39. C	49. A	59. D
10. B	20. D	30. C	40. A	50. D	60. A

TEST 2

DIRECTIONS: Each question or incomplete statement is followed by several suggested answers or completions. Select the one that BEST answers the question or completes the statement. *PRINT THE LETTER OF THE CORRECT ANSWER IN THE SPACE AT THE RIGHT.*

Questions 1-10.

DIRECTIONS: Questions 61 to 70 must be answered according to the INSTRUCTIONS FOR PARKING METER COLLECTORS and the COLLECTOR'S REPORT on Page 13.

INSTRUCTIONS FOP PARKING METER COLLECTORS

In his daily report, the collector shall list in the first column every meter from which he finds the coin box missing from the coin box housing, giving a clear statement of the reason therefor. In the middle column, he shall list every meter from which he cannot collect the coin box, giving a clear statement of the reason therefor. In the last column, he shall list every meter from which he does collect the coin box but in connection with which he finds some damage, defect, or other unusual condition either in the meter or in the parking space which should be reported.

To take a meter out of service, the collector is to put a hood over it. The word HOODED is to be used to indicate that a meter has been taken out of service by the collector. A meter which is restored to service by the collector removing the hood and putting an empty coin box into the coin box housing is to be reported in the middle column, the collector's report clearly indicating what was done.

The collector must always collect each coin box on his daily route that he can get to even if it contains no revenue. He must replace each coin box that he collects with a new coin box.

2 (#2)

Meter No.	Coin Box Missing	Meter No.	Coin Box Could Not Be Collected	Meter No.	Other Unusual Condition
102	Small crack in meter glass	110	Door wouldn't open - key broken off in lock	148	Lock jammed after coin box collected
135	Key would not fit in lock	117	No coin box in meter	159	No coin box in meter
140	Door open	122	Not collected	161	Meter glass covered with paint
145	Loose dimes near coin box -$1.00	130	Meter and pole removed	168	Cables left in parking space-hooded
15S	Hooded-parade	183	No revenue in coin box	173	Broken pavement in parking space-hooded
166	Door not locked	198	Parking space torn up	177	Meter found hooded for no apparent reason
167	Door jimmied	207	Coin box broken	181	No revenue
176	Lock broken -door open	216	Keyhole plugged	194	Timing mechanism out of order - hooded - box OK
189	Meter locked but no coin box in it	221	Vandalism -coin box collected	206	Not collected - meter covered by parade stands
202	Smashed -couldn't be opened	230	Meter would not unlock	210	Door wide open -3 dimes on pavement

1. Of the following meters, the one which MOST probably should have been reported in the column 'COIN BOX MISSING is   1.____

    A. 198   B. 183   C. 159   D. 148

2. Of the following meters, the one which most probably should NOT have been reported in the column COIN BOX COULD NOT BE COLLECTED is   2.____

    A. 230   B. 216   C. 207   D. 130

3. Of the following meters, the one which most probably should have been reported in the column OTHER UNUSUAL CONDITION is   3.____

    A. 110   B. 166   C. 189   D. 221

4. Of the following meters, the one which most probably should NOT have been reported in the column *COIN BOX MISSING* is

   A. 135   B. 140   C. 166   D. 176

5. Of the following meters, the one which most probably should HOT have been reported in the column *OTHER UNUSUAL CONDITION* is

   A. 168   B. 173   C. 177   D. 206

6. Of the following meters, the one which most probably was reported in the CORRECT column is

   A. 117   B. 153   C. 194   D. 202

7. Of the following meters, the one which most probably was reported in the WRONG column is

   A. 145   B. 161   C. 167   D. 181

8. Of the following meters, the one which most probably was reported in the CORRECT column is

   A. 102   B. 117   C. 148   D. 210

9. Of the following meters, the one which most probably was reported in the WRONG column is

   A. 123   B. 140   C. 202   D. 230

10. Of the following meters, the one which most probably has been INCOMPLETELY reported is

    A. 123   B. 176   C. 177   D. 216

11. A city has 51,489 parking meters. Thirteen percent of them require repairs. Therefore, the number of meters requiring repairs is MOST NEARLY

    A. 6,690   B. 6,695   C. 6,700   D. 6,705

12. The following sums of money were collected from parking meters in an eight-week period: $15,298, $14,248, $16,873, $18,137, $18,256, $19,342, $18,437, and $15,432. Therefore, the TOTAL amount collected from these meters for this eight-week period was MOST NEARLY

    A. $135,150   B. $135,985   C. $136,025   D. $136,543

13. There were 68,937 meters in operation at the end of December. Exactly one year later, there were 102,331 meters in operation.
    Therefore, the increase in the number of meters in operation is MOST NEARLY

    A. 34,400   B. 33,900   C. 33,400   D. 32,900

14. In a certain city, there are 24,482 parking meters. Of these meters, 3/8 are in Zone A. Therefore, the number of meters in Zone A is MOST NEARLY

    A. 3,060   B. 8,160   C. 9,180   D. 12,240

15. It costs $55,525 to service 9,995 parking meters. Therefore, the cost of servicing one meter is MOST NEARLY

    A. $2.50   B. $3.50   C. $4.50   D. $5.50

16. Of 165 parking meters, 0.14 of the total are out of order. Therefore, the number of these parking meters out of order is MOST NEARLY

    A. 83   B. 23   C. 8   D. 2.31

Question 17-26.

DIRECTIONS: Questions 77 to 86 must be answered according to the information given in the table below.

PARKING METER COLLECTIONS - CITY A

	Meter No.	Jan.	Feb.	March	April	Total
ZONE W	1062	$ 76.35	$89.30	$77.14	$ 86.16	$ 328.95
	1064	49.72	56.61	63.29	73.29	242.91
	1065	73.15	52.79	88.17	84.17	298.28
	1066	80.62	74.73	54.69	23.61	233.65
	TOTAL	$279.84	$273.43	$283.29	$267.23	$1103.79
ZONE X	769	$ 60.29	$50.27	$ 62.73	$ 76.53	$ 249.82
	770	81.40	73.12	70.51	40.27	265.30
	771	72.49	77.86	61.26	79.51	291.12
	772	65.14	62.40	70.91	72.26	270.71
	TOTAL	$279.32	$263.65	$265.41	$268.57	$1076.95
ZONE Y	815	$ 61.67	$60.96	$ 73.71	$ 68.92	$ 265.26
	816	41.92	44.63	46.17	47.74	180.46
	817	78.72	60.73	63.55	72.78	275.78
	TOTAL	$182.31	$166.32	$183.43	$189.44	$ 721.50
ZONE Z	963	$ 59.36	$63.53	$ 76.35	$ 76.35	$ 275.59
	964	42.53	40.IS	58.36	66.72	207.74
	965	77.72	63.27	70.37	80.15	291.51
	966	56.87	60.46	74.53	72.62	264.48
	967	62.35	59.50	60.29	59.62	241.76
	TOTAL	$298.83	$286.89	$339.90	$355.46	$1281.08

17. The parking meter zone which, on the average, collected MOST per meter for the four month period is Zone

    A. W   B. X   C. Y   D. Z

18. The two months in which the total collections in Zone X was more than $1\frac{1}{2}$ times but less than 2 times the total collections in Zone Y are   18.___

    A. January and February   B. January and March
    C. February and March   D. March and April

19. In March, there was more money collected than in February but less than in April in each zone EXCEPT Zone   19.___

    A. W   B. X   C. Y   D. Z

20. Parking meter number 770 was known to be out of order during part of one month. Judging only by the amount of collections, it is MOST likely that the month in which it was out of order is   20.___

    A. January   B. February   C. March   D. April

21. The greatest INCREASE in one month's total collections over the previous month occurred in Zone   21.___

    A. W   B. X   C. Y   D. Z

22. The greatest DECREASE in one month's total collections over the previous month occurred in Zone   22.___

    A. W   B. X   C. Y   D. Z

23. The month in which more than $175 but less than $300 was collected in each zone is   23.___

    A. January   B. February   C. March   D. April

24. The two parking meters which showed a steady monthly INCREASE in collections from January through April are   24.___

    A. 963 and 1064   B. 1064 and 816
    C. 966 and 816   D. 966 and 1064

25. The two parking meters which showed a steady monthly DECREASE in collections from January through April are   25.___

    A. 1066 and 770   B. 770 and 967
    C. 1066 and 967   D. 770 and 964

26. The parking meter from which the amount of money collected remained MOST NEARLY the same from month to month is   26.___

    A. 771   B. 967   C. 1063   D. 815

27. Suppose that a city block on a parking meter collector's route is 260 feet wide by 780 feet long.
    Therefore, the area of this block, in square feet, is MOST NEARLY   27.___

    A. 1,040   B. 2,080   C. 104,000   D. 203,000

28. The base of a container for coin boxes measures 2 feet by 3 feet. The base of the coin boxes measures 2 inches by 3 inches.
    The GREATEST number of coin boxes that will fit into the container in a single layer is   28.___

    A. 36   B. 72   C. 100   D. 144

29. The total collected from parking meters in City A for a twelve-month period was $701,790.
Therefore, the average collected per month for this twelvemonth period was MOST NEARLY

    A. $58,481 B. $58,483 C. $58,485 D. $8,421,480

30. It costs $158.46 each week to maintain the parking meters in a certain city.
Therefore, to maintain these meters for 372 weeks would cost MOST NEARLY

    A. $58,950 B. $58,975 C. $59,000 D. $59,025

KEY (CORRECT ANSWERS)

1. C	11. B	21. D
2. C	12. C	22. A
3. D	13. C	23. A
4. A	14. C	24. B
5. D	15. D	25. A
6. C	16. B	26. B
7. A	17. A	27. D
8. C	18. A	28. D
9. C	19. A	29. B
10. A	20. D	30. A

EXAMINATION SECTION
TEST 1

DIRECTIONS: Each question or incomplete statement is followed by several suggested answers or completions. Select the one that BEST answers the question or completes the statement. *PRINT THE LETTER OF THE CORRECT ANSWER IN THE SPACE AT THE RIGHT.*

1. It is a good idea to have parking meter attendants wear uniforms MAINLY because uniforms would

    A. build morale, especially in a new group of employees
    B. identify parking meter attendants on duty to the public
    C. insure proper clothing for outdoor work
    D. show the importance of the parking meter attendants

    1.____

2. If a passerby asks you how many parking tickets the City issued last year, you should

    A. advise him that such information cannot be made public
    B. ask him why he wants this information
    C. refer him to the main office of the Traffic Department
    D. tell him how many tickets you issued last month

    2.____

3. Just after you have ticketed a car for a parking violation, the driver shows up and becomes very angry.
   Of the following, the BEST thing for you to do is to

    A. listen until he calms down and then politely explain why you ticketed his car
    B. walk away immediately before he uses bad language
    C. warn him that an angry motorist is more likely to get into an accident
    D. whistle for a policeman to arrest him

    3.____

4. If a parking meter attendant on duty becomes too sick to continue working, she should FIRST

    A. advise her supervisor
    B. go home
    C. have a cup of coffee in the nearest restaurant
    D. patrol her area more slowly to see if she'll feel better

    4.____

5. A City employee who is driving a City-owned vehicle

    A. does not have to observe certain driving regulations
    B. does not have to observe the City's parking regulations
    C. should observe every driving and parking regulation
    D. should observe every driving regulation but not all parking regulations

    5.____

6. Your supervisor has asked the parking meter attendants in her section to try out a new system for making out daily reports.
   Suppose that you do not think the system is necessary. You should

    A. use the new system even though you don't think the change is necessary
    B. go on using the old system
    C. make out no reports until the supervisor decides on a final system
    D. write a complaint to the department head that the new system is unnecessary

    6.____

7. If a passerby criticizes you for ticketing a car and asks for your name and number, you should

   A. give him your name and number
   B. give him your supervisor's name
   C. pay no attention to him and report the incident to your supervisor
   D. tell him it is not his job but yours

8. Suppose that during patrol of your post you come upon an old man with blood on his face, seated on the sidewalk leaning against the tire of a parked car.
   Of the following, the best action for you to take FIRST is to

   A. ask the man for identification
   B. call a policeman to move him from his dangerous position
   C. examine him to see what first aid help you can give
   D. look up and down the block to find a witness to the accident

9. An attempt to prevent an enforcement agent from performing her duty is BEST defined as

   A. blackmailing   B. compounding a felony
   C. conspiracy   D. obstructing justice

10. If Unit R was established before Unit K, and Unit K was established before Unit T, then it would be MOST correct to say that

    A. Unit K was established before Unit R
    B. Unit T was established before Unit R
    C. Unit K was established after Unit T
    D. Unit T was established after Unit R

Questions 11-20

DIRECTIONS: In Questions 11 to 20, there are five pairs of numbers or letters and numbers. Compare each pair and decide how many pairs are EXACTLY ALIKE. In the space at the right, mark the letter

      A. if only one pair is exactly alike
      B. if only two pairs are exactly alike
      C. if only three pairs are exactly alike
      D. if only four pairs are exactly alike
      E. if all five pairs are exactly alike

11. 73-F F-73
    FF-73   ....   FF-73
    F-7373   ....   F-7373
    373-FF 337-FF
    F-733   ....   337-F

12. 3NY-56   ....   3NY-65
    5NY-356   ....   3NY-356
    6NY-3566   ....   3NY-3566
    5NY-6536   ....   5NY-6536
    3NY-5663   ....   5NY-3663

3 (#1)

13.	0-17158	....	0-17158	13.____
	0-71518	....	0-71518	
	0-11758	....	0-11758	
	0-15817	....	0-15817	
	0-51178	....	0-51178	
14.	COB-065	....	COB-065	14.____
	BCL-506	....	BCL-506	
	LBC-650	....	LBC-650	
	DLB-560	....	DLB-560	
	CDB-056	....	COB-065	
15.	1A-7908	....	1A-7908	15.____
	7A-8901	....	7A-8091	
	7A-891	....	7A-891	
	1A-9078	....	1A-9708	
	9A-7018	....	9A-7081	
16.	4KQ-9130	....	4KQ-9130	16.____
	4KQ-9310	....	4KQ-9130	
	4KQ-9031	....	4KQ-9031	
	4KQ-9301	...	4KQ-9301	
	4KQ-9013	....	4KQ-9013	
17.	2V-6426	....	2V-6246	17.____
	2N-6246	....	2N-6246	
	2V-6426	....	2N-6426	
	2N-6624	....	2N-6624	
	2V-6462	....	2V-6462	
18.	MK-89	....	MK-98	18.____
	98-MK	....	89-MK	
	MSK-998	....	MSK-998	
	MOSK	....	MOKS	
	SMK-899	....	SMK-899	
19.	8MD-2104	....	8MD-2014	19.____
	2MD-8140	....	2MD-8140	
	814-MD	....	814-MD	
	4MD-8201	....	4MD-8201	
	MD-28	....	MD-481	
20.	161-035	....	161-035	20.____
	150-316	....	150-316	
	315-160	....	315-160	
	131-650	....	131-650	
	165-301	....	165-301	

21. When you extend your left hand and arm downward while driving a car, you are signaling to the car behind that you are going to

    A. make a left turn
    B. make a right turn
    C. pass the car on your right
    D. slow down or stop

22. In North America, the words *Yield Right of Way* appear on signs shaped like

    A. (pentagon) B. (diamond) C. (circle) D. (octagon)

23. A *No Standing* sign posted at the curb means that

    A. only buses may stop here
    B. passenger cars may not stop here for any reason
    C. trucks may unload merchandise here
    D. vehicles may stop here only to take on or let out passengers

24. As the traffic light changes from red to green, a pedestrian starts to cross against the light in front of the vehicle you are driving.
    Of the following, the BEST thing for you to do is to

    A. blow your horn several times to warn the pedestrian
    B. let the pedestrian cross before moving your vehicle
    C. race your motor to hurry the pedestrian across
    D. wave to the pedestrian to get back on the curb

25. The BEST practice when driving on a city highway where the posted speed limit is 30 miles is to

    A. drive at a speed a couple of miles under the speed limit for maximum safety
    B. drive no more than 5 miles faster than the posted limit if traffic conditions permit
    C. keep up with the traffic within the posted speed limit
    D. maintain a steady pace of 30 miles an hour at all times

26. A supervisor notices that one of her employees is trying very hard to do a good job but seems to lack the necessary skills to do the work properly.
    In order to help this employee do better work, it would be BEST for the supervisor to

    A. allow the employee to *learn by doing*
    B. give the employee easier work to do
    C. give the employee more training
    D. set lower production quotas for this employee

27. While you are explaining a new procedure to your employees at a staff meeting, one of them asks a question about the procedure which you can't answer.
The MOST appropriate action for you to take is to

   A. admit you don't know the answer and promise to get the information
   B. ask the employee why she wants the information before you give an answer
   C. ask the other employees present to try to answer the question
   D. pay no attention to the question and continue with your explanation

28. When all of her employees are assigned to perform identical routine tasks, a supervisor would probably find it MOST difficult to differentiate among these employees as to the

   A. amount of work each completes
   B. initiative each one shows in doing the work
   C. number of errors in each one's work
   D. number of times each one is absent or late

29. The one of the following guiding principles to which a supervisor should give the GREATEST weight when it becomes necessary to discipline an employee is that the

   A. discipline should be of such a nature as to improve the future work of the employee
   B. main benefit gained in disciplining one employee is that all employees are kept from breaking the same rule
   C. morale of all the employees should be improved by the discipline of the one
   D. rules should be applied in a fixed and unchanging manner

30. In using praise to encourage employees to do better work, the supervisor should realize that praising an employee too often is not good MAINLY because the

   A. employee will be resented by her fellow employees
   B. employee will begin to think she's doing too much work
   C. praise will lose its value as an incentive
   D. supervisor doesn't have the time to praise an employee frequently

31. A supervisor notices that one of her best employees has apparently begun to loaf on the job.
In this situation, the supervisor should FIRST

   A. allow the employee a period of grace in view of her excellent record
   B. change the employee's job assignment
   C. determine the reason for the change in the employee's behavior
   D. take disciplinary action immediately as she would with any other employee

32. A supervisor who wants to get a spirit of friendly cooperation from the employees in her unit is MOST likely to be successful if she

   A. makes no exceptions in strictly enforcing department procedures
   B. shows a cooperative spirit herself
   C. tells them they are the best in the department
   D. treats them to coffee once in a while

33. *Accidents do not just happen.*
    In view of this statement, it is important for the supervisor to realize that

    A. accidents are sometimes deliberate
    B. combinations of unavoidable circumstances cause accidents
    C. she must take the blame for each accident
    D. she should train her employees in accident prevention

34. Suppose your superior points out to you several jobs that were poorly done by the employees under your supervision. As the supervisor of these employees, you should

    A. accept responsibility for the poor work and take steps to improve the work in the future
    B. blame the employees for shirking on the job while you were busy on other work
    C. defend the employees since up to this time they were all good workers
    D. explain that the poor work was due to circumstances beyond your control

35. If a supervisor discovers a situation which is a possible source of grievance, it would be BEST for her to

    A. be ready to answer the employees when they make a direct complaint
    B. do nothing until the employees make a direct complaint
    C. tell the employees, in order to keep them from making a direct complaint, that nothing can be done
    D. try to remove the cause before the employees make a direct complaint

36. Suppose there is a departmental rule that requires supervisors to prepare reports of unusual incidents by the end of the tour of duty in which the incident occurs.
    The MAIN reason for requiring such prompt recording is that

    A. a quick decision can be made whether the employee involved was neglectful of her duty
    B. other required reports cannot be made out until this one is turned in
    C. the facts are recorded before they are forgotten or confused by those involved in the incident
    D. the report is submitted before the supervisor required to make the report may possibly leave the department

37. Suppose that one of your employees is accidentally injured on the job.
    In your report on the accident, it is LEAST important to include the

    A. employee's general attitude toward the department
    B. kind of injury and parts of the body involved
    C. kind of work the employee was doing when the accident happened
    D. time and place of the accident

38. Of the following duties connected with the preparation of official reports, the one which the Senior Parking Meter Attendant should USUALLY do herself rather than have one of her subordinates do is

    A. entering numerical data on official reports
    B. planning the preparation and submission of official reports
    C. proofreading official reports after they are typed
    D. securing from original sources data needed for the official report

39. Periodic reports are usually submitted on printed report forms instead of by means of individually written reports. Of the following, the CHIEF advantage of using a uniform printed report form for periodic reports is that

   A. anyone can prepare the report
   B. needed information is less likely to be omitted from the report
   C. promptness in submitting the report is assured
   D. unusual incidents can be reported fully

40. Assume that your superior asked you to conduct a study of the parking situation in a certain area and to recommend necessary changes in the parking meter program. After your study, you submit a fairly long report.
The one of the following sections which should be included in the introduction to this report is a

   A. brief answer to possible objections to your recommendations
   B. complete statement of the advantages to be gained from your recommendations
   C. plan for putting your recommendations into operation
   D. summary of the conclusions you reached

KEY (CORRECT ANSWERS)

1. B	11. B	21. D	31. C
2. C	12. A	22. A	32. B
3. A	13. E	23. D	33. D
4. A	14. D	24. B	34. A
5. C	15. B	25. C	35. D
6. A	16. D	26. C	36. C
7. A	17. C	27. A	37. A
8. C	18. B	28. B	38. B
9. D	19. C	29. A	39. B
10. D	20. E	30. C	40. D

MAP READING
EXAMINATION SECTION
TEST 1

DIRECTIONS: Each question or incomplete statement is followed by several suggested answers or completions. Select the one that BEST answers the question or completes the Statement. *PRINT THE LETTER OF THE CORRECT ANSWER IN THE SPACE AT THE RIGHT.*

Questions 1-5.

DIRECTIONS: Questions 1 through 5 are to be answered SOLELY on the basis of the following information and map.

An employee may be required to assist civilians who seek travel directions or referral to city agencies and facilities.

The following is a map of part of a city, where several public offices and other institutions are located. Each of the squares represents one city block. Street names are as shown. If there is an arrow next to the street name, it means the street is one-way only in the direction of the arrow. If there is no arrow next to the street name, two-way traffic is allowed.

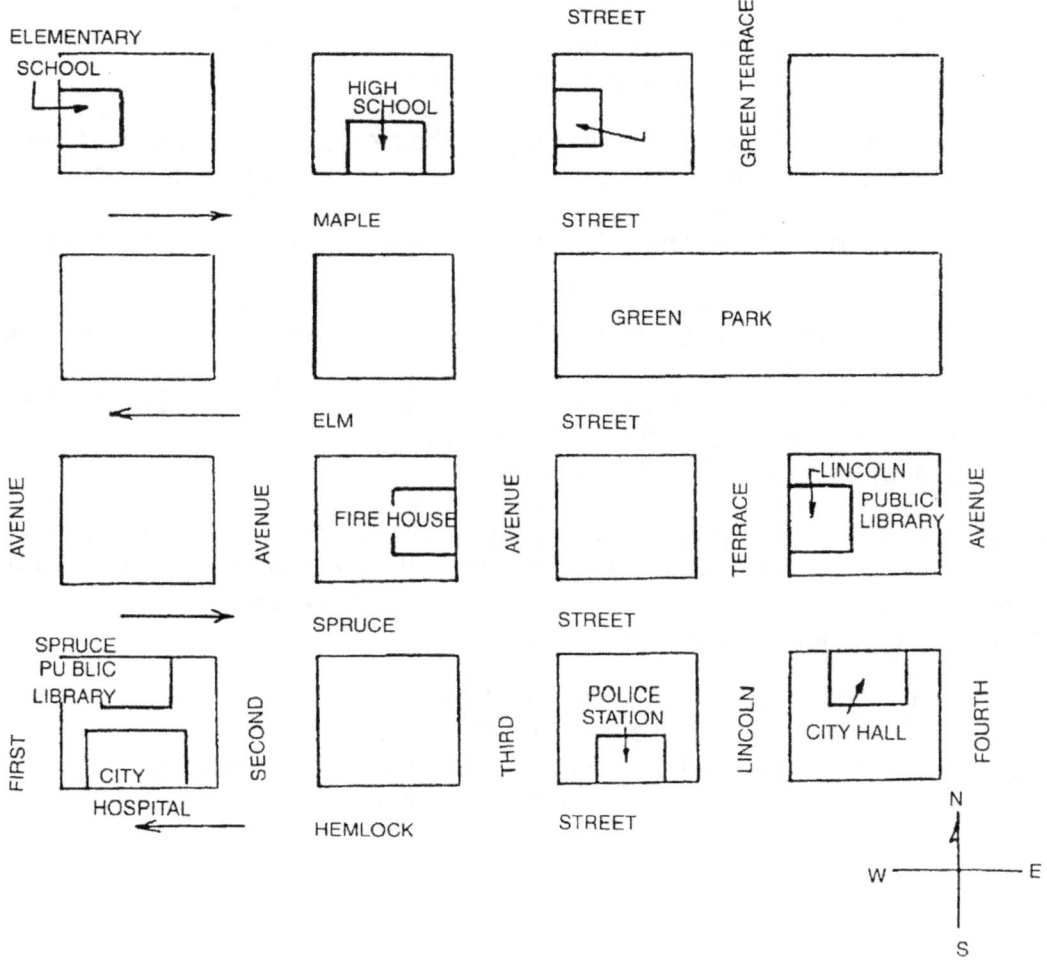

55

1. A woman whose handbag was stolen from her in Green Park asks a firefighter at the firehouse where to go to report the crime.
   The firefighter should tell the woman to go to the

   A. police station on Spruce Street
   B. police station on Hemlock Street
   C. city hall on Spruce Street
   D. city hall on Hemlock Street

2. A disabled senior citizen who lives on Green Terrace telephones the firehouse to ask which library is closest to her home.
   The firefighter should tell the senior citizen it is the

   A. Spruce Public Library on Lincoln Terrace
   B. Lincoln Public Library on Spruce Street
   C. Spruce Public Library on Spruce Street
   D. Lincoln Public Library on Lincoln Terrace

3. A woman calls the firehouse to ask for the exact location of City Hall.
   She should be told that it is on

   A. Hemlock Street, between Lincoln Terrace and Fourth Avenue
   B. Spruce Street, between Lincoln Terrace and Fourth Avenue
   C. Lincoln Terrace, between Spruce Street and Elm Street
   D. Green Terrace, between Maple Street and Pine Street

4. A delivery truck driver is having trouble finding the high school to make a delivery. The driver parks the truck across from the firehouse on Third Avenue facing north and goes into the firehouse to ask directions.
   In giving directions, the firefighter should tell the driver to go _____ to the school.

   A. north on Third Avenue to Pine Street and then make a right
   B. south on Third Avenue, make a left on Hemlock Street, and then make a right on Second Avenue
   C. north on Third Avenue, turn left on Elm Street, make a right on Second Avenue and go to Maple Street, then make another right
   D. north on Third Avenue to Maple Street, and then make a left

5. A man comes to the firehouse accompanied by his son and daughter. He wants to register his son in the high school and his daughter in the elementary school. He asks a firefighter which school is closest for him to walk to from the firehouse.
   The firefighter should tell the man that the

   A. high school is closer than the elementary school
   B. elementary school is closer than the high school
   C. elementary school and high school are the same distance away
   D. elementary school and high school are in opposite directions

Questions 6-8.

DIRECTIONS: Questions 6 through 8 are to be answered SOLELY on the basis of the following map and information. The flow of traffic is indicated by the arrows. If there is only one arrow shown, then traffic flows in the direction indicated by the arrow. If there are two arrows, then traffic flows in both directions. You must follow the flow of traffic

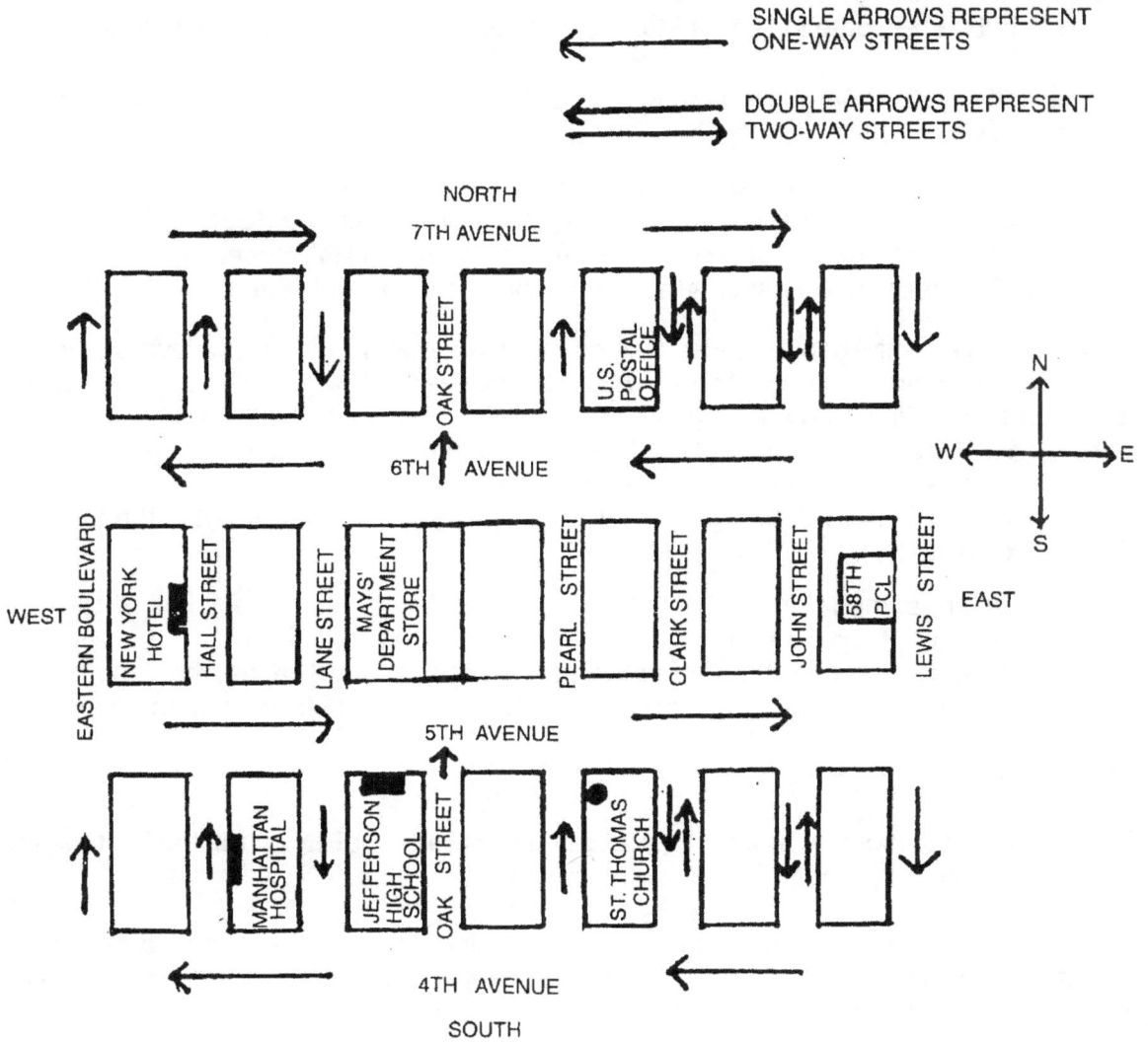

6. Traffic Enforcement Agent Fox was on foot patrol at John Street between 6th and 7th Avenues when a motorist driving southbound asked her for directions to the New York Hotel, which is located on Hall Street between 5th and 6th Avenues. Which one of the following is the SHORTEST route for Agent Fox to direct the motorist to take, making sure to obey all traffic regulations?
Travel _____ to the New York Hotel.

   A. north on John Street, then east on 7th Avenue, then north on Lewis Street, then west on 4th Avenue, then north on Eastern Boulevard, then east on 5th Avenue, then north on Hall Street
   B. south on John Street, then west on 6th Avenue, then south on Eastern Boulevard, then east on 5th Avenue, then north on Hall Street

C. south on John Street, then west on 6th Avenue, then south on Clark Street, then east on 4th Avenue, then north on Eastern Boulevard, then east on 5th Avenue, then north on Hall Street
D. south on John Street, then west on 4th Avenue, then north on Hall Street

7. Traffic Enforcement Agent Murphy is on motorized patrol on 7th Avenue between Oak Street and Pearl Street when Lt. Robertson radios him to go to Jefferson High School, located on 5th Avenue between Lane Street and Oak Street. Which one of the following is the SHORTEST route for Agent Murphy to take, making sure to obey all the traffic regulations?
Travel east on 7th Avenue, then south on _____, then east on 5th Avenue to Jefferson High School.

   A. Clark Street, then west on 4th Avenue, then north on Hall Street
   B. Pearl Street, then west on 4th Avenue, then north on Lane Street
   C. Lewis Street, then west on 6th Avenue, then south on Hall Street
   D. Lewis Street, then west on 4th Avenue, then north on Oak Street

8. Traffic Enforcement Agent Vasquez was on 4th Avenue and Eastern Boulevard when a motorist asked him for directions to the 58th Police Precinct, which is located on Lewis Street between 5th and 6th Avenues.
Which one of the following is the SHORTEST route for Agent Vasquez to direct the motorist to take, making sure to obey all traffic regulations.
Travel north on Eastern Boulevard, then east on _____ on Lewis Street to the 58th Police Precinct.

   A. 5th Avenue, then north
   B. 7th Avenue, then south
   C. 6th Avenue, then north on Pearl Street, then east on 7th Avenue, then south
   D. 5th Avenue, then north on Clark Street, then east on 6th Avenue, then south

Questions 9-13.

DIRECTIONS: Questions 9 through 13 are to be answered SOLELY on the basis of the following map and the following information.

Toll collectors answer motorists' questions concerning directions by reading a map of the metropolitan area. Although many alternate routes leading to destinations exist on the following map, you are to choose the MOST direct route of those given.

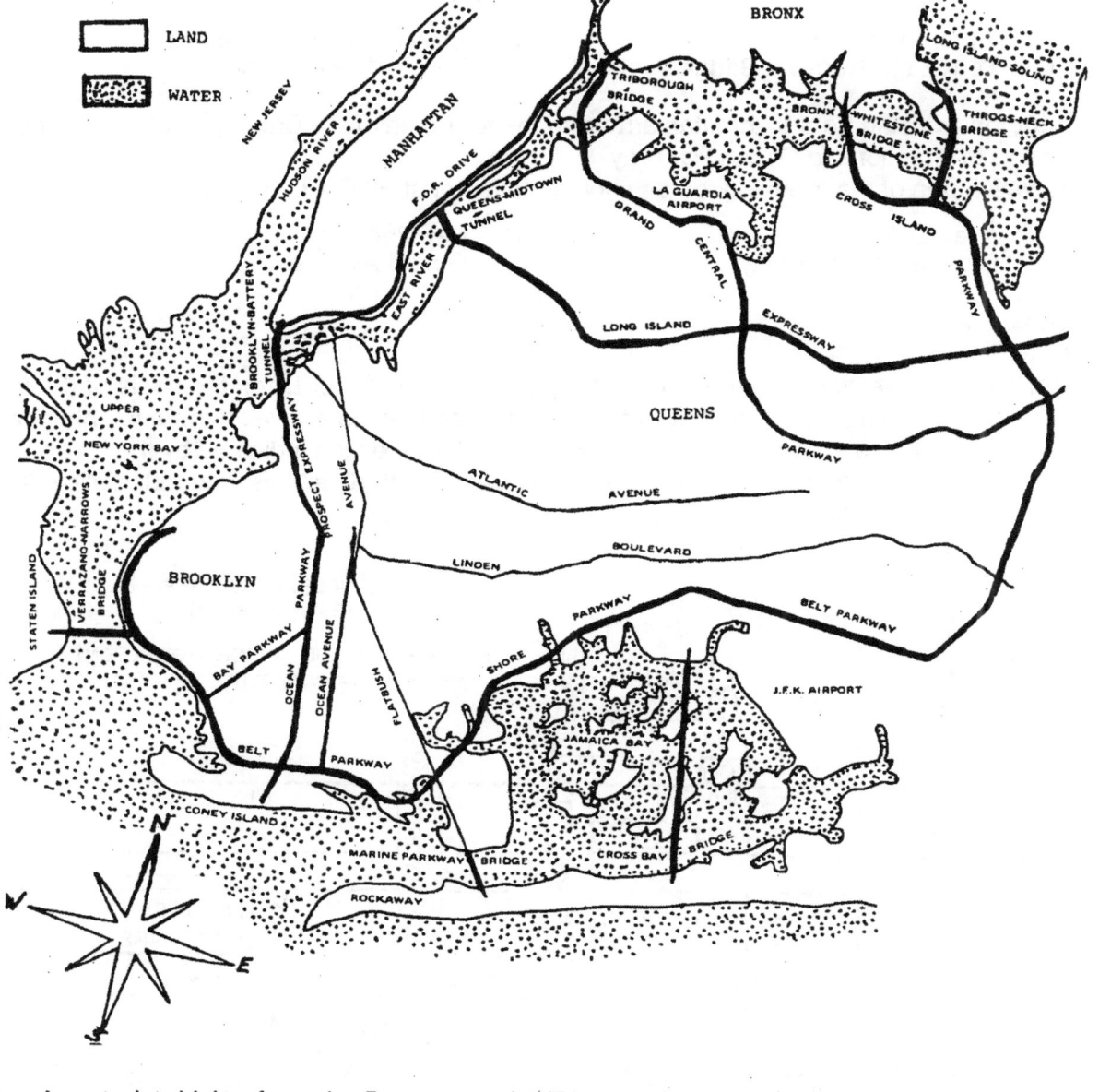

9. A motorist driving from the Bronx over the Triborough Bridge wants to go to LaGuardia Airport in Queens.
   The officer should direct him to

   A. Grand Central Parkway
   B. F.D.R. Drive
   C. Shore Parkway
   D. Flatbush Avenue

10. A motorist driving from Manhattan through the Queens Midtown Tunnel would travel DIRECTLY onto

    A. Shore Parkway
    B. F.D.R. Drive
    C. Long Island Expressway
    D. Atlantic Avenue

11. A motorist traveling north over the Marine Parkway Bridge should take which route to reach Coney Island?

    A. Shore Parkway East
    B. Belt Parkway West
    C. Linden Boulevard
    D. Ocean Parkway

12. Which facility does NOT connect the Bronx and Queens?

    A. Triborough Bridge
    B. Bronx-Whitestone Bridge
    C. Verrazano-Narrows Bridge
    D. Throgs-Neck Bridge

13. A motorist driving from Manhattan arrives at the toll booth of the Brooklyn-Battery Tunnel and asks directions to Ocean Parkway.
    To which one of the following routes should the motorist FIRST be directed?

    A. Atlantic Avenue
    B. Bay Parkway
    C. Prospect Expressway
    D. Ocean Avenue

Questions 14-16.

DIRECTIONS: Questions 14 through 16 are to be answered SOLELY on the basis of the following map. The flow of traffic is indicated by the arrows. If there is only one arrow shown, then traffic flows only in the direction indicated by the arrow. If there are two arrows, then traffic flows in both directions. You must follow the flow of traffic.

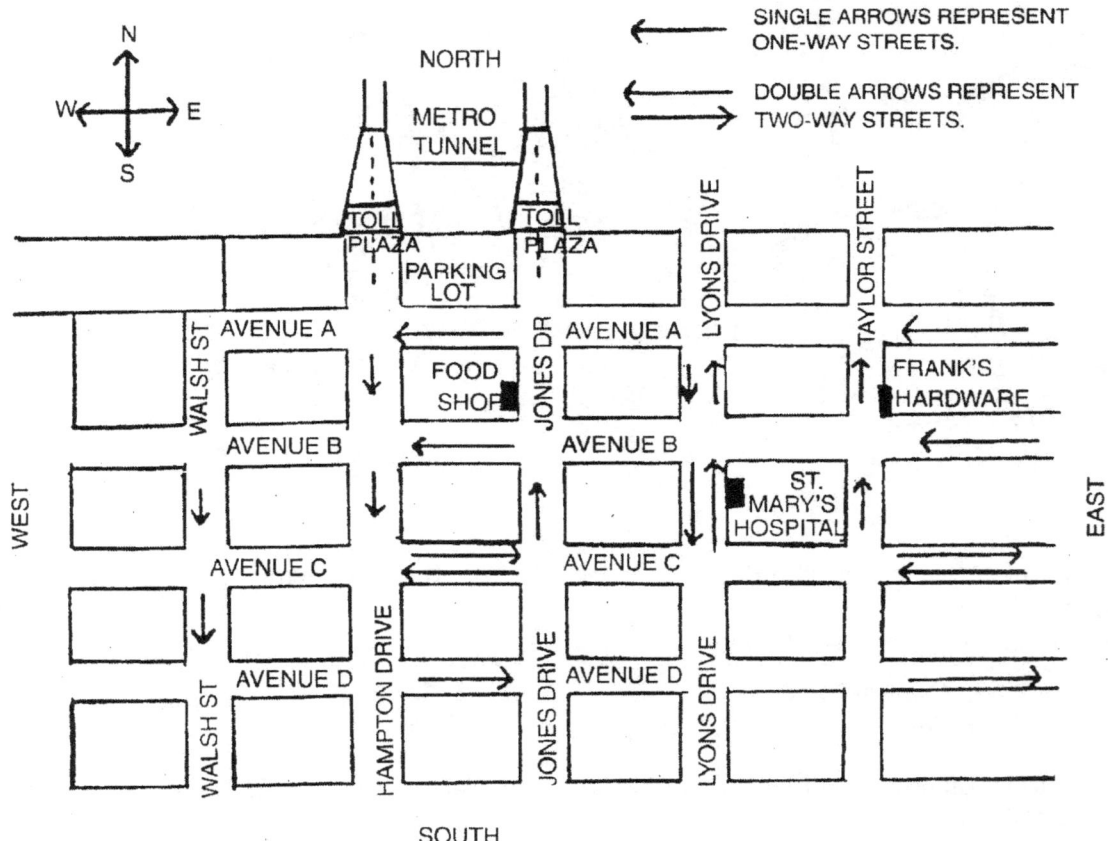

14. A motorist is exiting the Metro Tunnel and approaches the bridge and tunnel officer at the toll plaza. He asks the officer how to get to the food shop on Jones Drive. Which one of the following is the SHORTEST route for the motorist to take, making sure to obey all traffic regulations?
    Travel south on Hampton Drive, then left on _____ on Jones Drive to the food shop.

A. Avenue A, then right
B. Avenue B, then right
C. Avenue D, then left
D. Avenue C, then left

15. A motorist heading south pulls up to a toll booth at the exit of the Metro Tunnel and asks Bridge and Tunnel Officer Evans how to get to Frank's Hardware Store on Taylor Street. Which one of the following is the SHORTEST route for the motorist to take, making sure to obey all traffic regulations?
Travel south on Hampton Drive, then east on

   A. Avenue B to Taylor Street
   B. Avenue D, then north on Taylor Street to Avenue B
   C. Avenue C, then north on Taylor Street to Avenue B
   D. Avenue C, then north on Lyons Drive, then east on Avenue B to Taylor Street

15._____

16. A motorist is exiting the Metro Tunnel and approaches the toll plaza. She asks Bridge and Tunnel Officer Owens for directions to St. Mary's Hospital. Which one of the following is the SHORTEST route for the motorist to take, making sure to obey all traffic regulations?
Travel south on Hampton Drive, then _____ on Lyons Drive to St. Mary's Hospital.

   A. left on Avenue D, then left
   B. right on Avenue A, then left on Walsh Street, then left on Avenue D, then left
   C. left on Avenue C, then left
   D. left on Avenue B, then right

16._____

Questions 17-18.

DIRECTIONS: Questions 17 and 18 are to be answered SOLELY on the basis of the map which appears on the following page. The flow of traffic is indicated by the arrows. If there is only one arrow shown, then traffic flows only in the direction indicated by the arrow. If there are two arrows shown, then traffic flows in both directions. You must follow the flow of traffic.

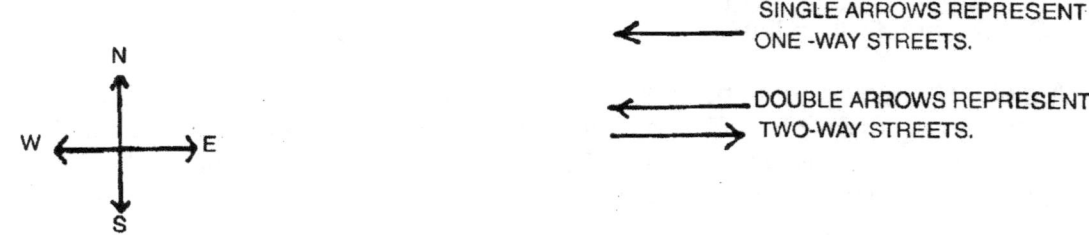

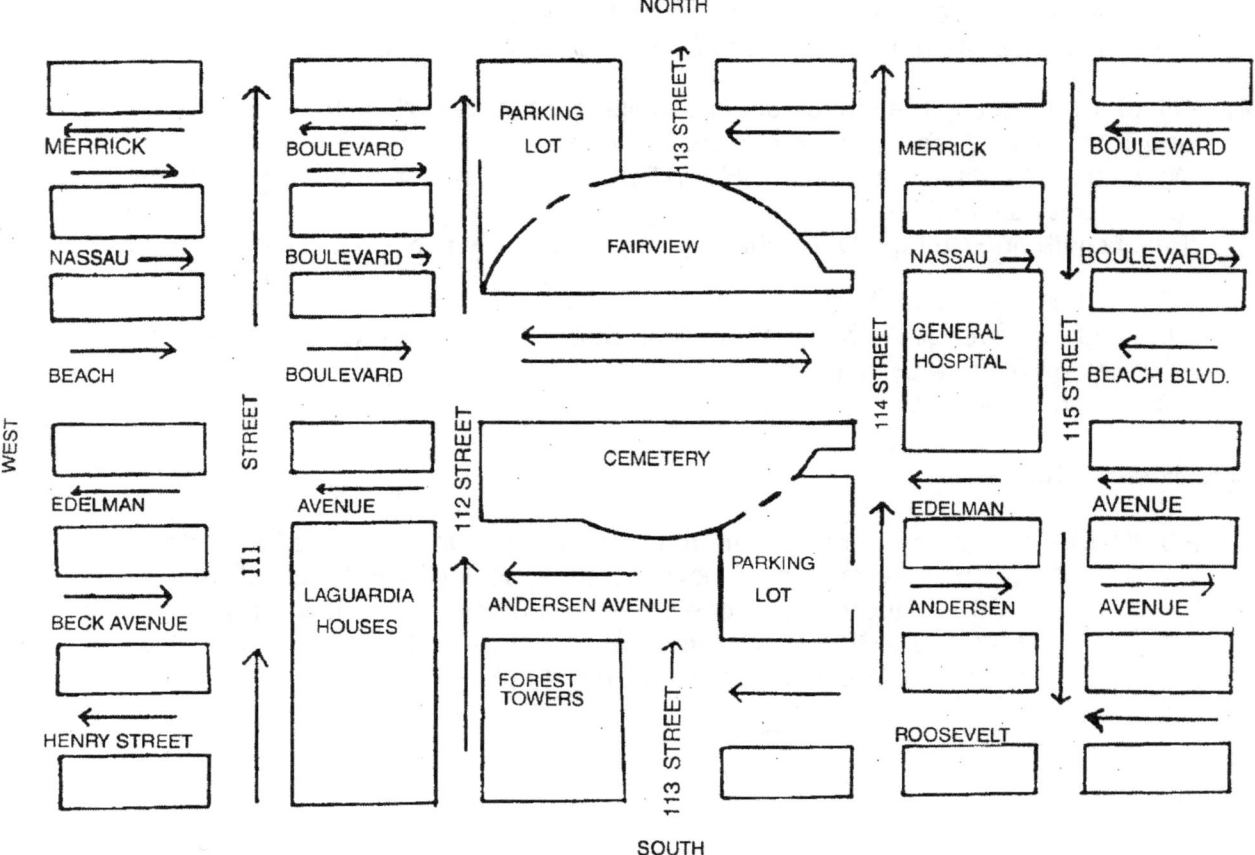

17. Police Officers Glenn and Albertson are on 111th Street at Henry Street when they are dispatched to a past robbery at Beach Boulevard and 115th Street.
Which one of the following is the SHORTEST route for the officers to follow in their patrol car, making sure to obey all traffic regulations?
Travel north on 111th Street, then east on _____ south on 115th Street.

    A. Edelman Avenue, then north on 112th Street, then east on Beach Boulevard, then north on 114th Street, then east on Nassau Boulevard, then one block
    B. Beach Boulevard, then north on 114th Street, then east on Nassau Boulevard, then one block
    C. Merrick Boulevard, then two blocks
    D. Nassau Boulevard, then south on 112th Street, then east on Beach Boulevard, then north on 114th Street, then east on Nassau Boulevard, then one block

17._____

18. Later in their tour, Officers Glenn and Albertson are driving on 114th Street. If they make a left turn to enter the parking lot at Andersen Avenue, and then make a u-turn, in what direction would they now be headed?

    A. North   B. South   C. East   D. West

18.____

Questions 19-20.

DIRECTIONS: Questions 19 and 20 are to be answered SOLELY on the basis of the following map. The flow of traffic is indicated by the arrows. If there is only one arrow shown, then traffic flows only in the direction indicated by the arrow. If there are two arrows shown, then traffic flows in both directions. You must follow the flow of traffic.

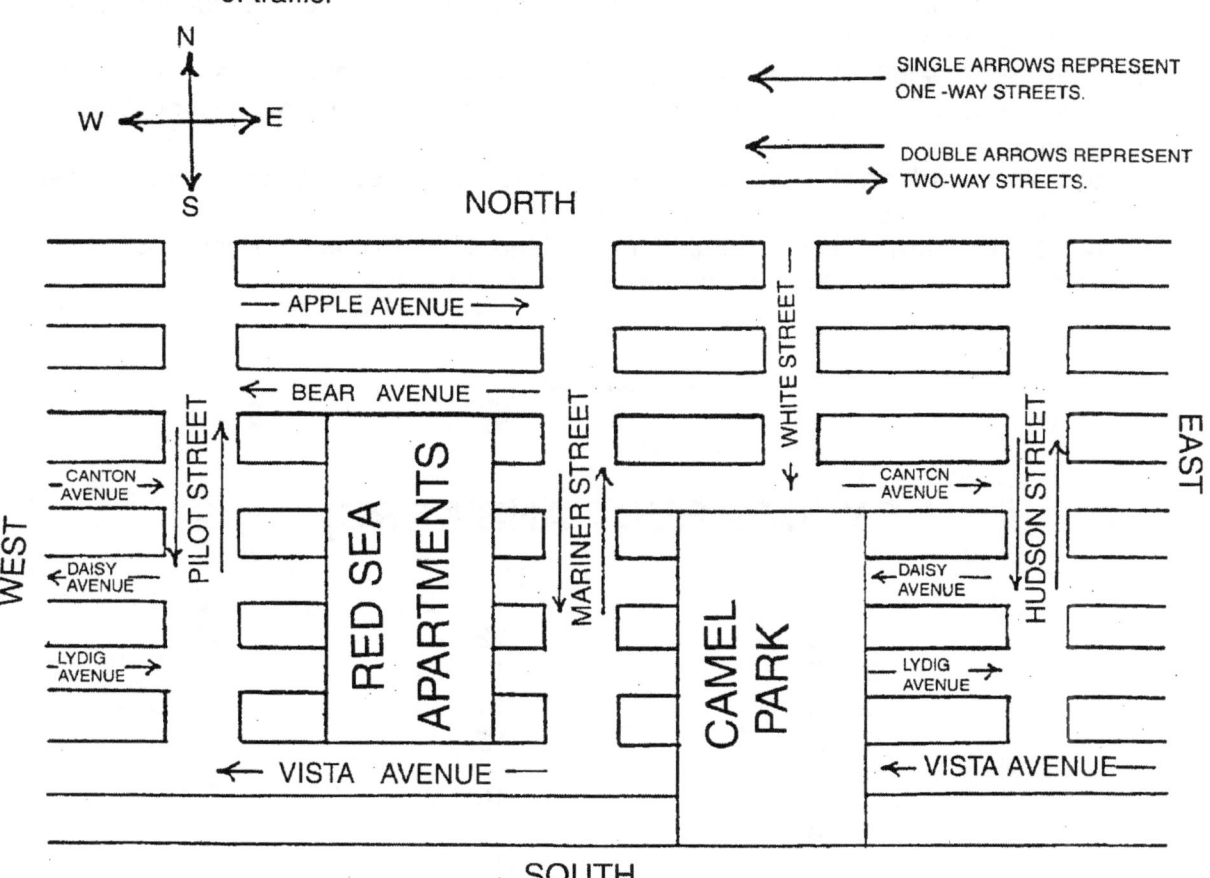

19. You are located at Apple Avenue and White Street. You receive a call to respond to the corner of Lydig Avenue and Pilot Street.
Which one of the following is the MOST direct route for you to take in your patrol car, making sure to obey all traffic regulations?
Travel _____ on Pilot Street.

    A. two blocks south on White Street, then one block east on Canton Avenue, then one block north on Hudson Street, then three blocks west on Bear Avenue, then three blocks south

    B. one block south on White Street, then two blocks west on Bear Avenue, then three blocks south

19.____

C. two blocks west on Apple Avenue, then four blocks south
D. two blocks south on White Street, then one block west on Canton Avenue, then three blocks south on Mariner Street, then one block west on Vista Avenue, then one block north

20. You are located at Canton Avenue and Pilot Street. You receive a call of a crime in progress at the intersection of Canton Avenue and Hudson Street.
Which one of the following is the MOST direct route for you to take in your patrol car, making sure to obey all traffic regulations?
Travel

   A. two blocks north on Pilot Street, then two blocks east on Apple Avenue, then one block south on White Street, then one block east on Bear Avenue, then one block south on Hudson Street
   B. three blocks south on Pilot Street, then travel one block east on Vista Avenue, then travel three blocks north on Mariner Street, then travel two blocks east on Canton Avenue
   C. one block north on Pilot Street, then travel three blocks east on Bear Avenue, then travel one block south on Hudson Street
   D. two blocks north on Pilot Street, then travel three blocks east on Apple Avenue, then travel two blocks south on Hudson Street

20. ____

KEY (CORRECT ANSWERS)

1.	B	11.	B/D
2.	D	12.	C
3.	B	13.	C
4.	C	14.	D
5.	A	15.	C
6.	D	16.	C
7.	A	17.	B
8.	B	18.	C
9.	A	19.	B
10.	C	20.	D

INTERPRETING STATISTICAL DATA GRAPHS, CHARTS AND TABLES

EXAMINATION SECTION
TEST 1

DIRECTIONS: Each question or incomplete statement is followed by several suggested answers or completions. Select the one that BEST answers the question or completes the statement. *PRINT THE LETTER OF THE CORRECT ANSWER IN THE SPACE AT THE RIGHT.*

Questions 1-4.

DIRECTIONS: Questions 1 through 4 are to be answered SOLELY on the basis of the chart below which provides information about the current assignments of a group of agents.

Name of Agent	Code No. of Assignment	Date Assigned	Section No.	Name of Supervisor
Estes, Jerome	34-08-A	10/8/18	F0281	H. Landon
Gomez, Margie	34-07-A	10/15/18	F0281	S. Lee
Isaac, John	32-07-B	10/8/18	F0381	R. Puente
Kaplan, Pearl	32-07-A	11/5/18	F0381	R. Puente
Kapler, Peter	34-05-A	10/22/18	F0281	S. Lee
Karell, Peter	42-05-A	11/12/18	F1281	T. Pujol

1. Two of the agents received their current assignments on the same date. This date is _____, 2018.

   A. October 8 B. October 15
   C. October 22 D. November 12

2. Which of the following is Peter Kapler's section number?

   A. 34-05-A B. 42-05-A C. F0281 D. F1281

3. R. Puente is the supervisor for

   A. John Isaac *only*
   B. John Isaac and Pearl Kaplan
   C. John Isaac, Pearl Kaplan, and Peter Kapler
   D. John Isaac, Pearl Kaplan, and Peter Karell

4. How many of the agents were given their current assignments BEFORE November 1, 2018?

   A. 2 B. 4 C. 5 D. 6

1.___
2.___
3.___
4.___

KEY (CORRECT ANSWERS)

1. A
2. C
3. B
4. B

TEST 2

Questions 1-10.

DIRECTIONS: Questions 1 through 10 are to be answered on the basis of the INSTRUCTIONS FOR PARKING METER COLLECTORS and the COLLECTOR'S REPORT given below.

INSTRUCTIONS FOR PARKING METER COLLECTORS.

In his daily report, the collector shall list in the first column every meter from which he finds the coin box missing from the coin box housing, giving a clear statement of the reason therefor. In the middle column, he shall list every meter from which he cannot collect the coin box, giving a clear statement of the reason therefor. In the last column, he shall list every meter from which he does collect the coin box but in connection with which he finds some damage, defect or other unusual condition either in the meter or in the parking space which should be reported.

To take a meter out of service, the collector is to put a hood over it. The word *HOODED* is to be used to indicate that a meter has been taken out of service by the collector. A meter which is restored to service by the collector removing the hood and putting an empty coin box into the coin box housing is to be reported in the middle column, the collector's report clearly indicating what was done.

The collector must always collect each coin box on his daily route that he can get to even if it contains no revenue. He must replace each coin box that he collects with a new coin box.

COLLECTOR'S REPORT

Meter No.	Coin Box Missing	Meter No.	Coin Box Could Not Be Collected	Meter No.	Other Unusual Condition
102	Small crack in meter glass	110	Door wouldn't open-key broken off in lock	148	Lock jammed after coin box collected
135	Key would not fit in lock	117	No coin box in meter	159	No coin box in meter
140	Door open	123	Not collected	161	Meter glass covered with paint
145	Loose quarters near coin box - $1.00	130	Meter and pole removed	168	Cables left in parking space-hooded
153	Hooded-parade	183	No revenue in coin box	173	Broken pavement in parking space-hooded
166	Door not locked	198	Parking space torn up	177	Meter found hooded for no apparent reason
167	Door jimmied	207	Coin box broken	181	No revenue
176	Lock broken -door open	216	Keyhole plugged	194	Timing mechanism out of order-hooded-box O.K.

2 (#2)

| 189 | Meter locked but no coin box in it | 221 | Vandalism- coin box collected | 206 | Not collected-meter covered by parade stands |
| 202 | Smashed-couldn't be opened | 230 | Meter would not unlock | 210 | Door wide open- 3 quarters on pavement |

1. Of the following meters, the one which MOST probably should have been reported in the column COIN BOX MISSING is

   A. 198   B. 183   C. 159   D. 148

2. Of the following meters, the one which MOST probably should NOT have been reported in the column COIN BOX COULD NOT BE COLLECTED is

   A. 230   B. 216   C. 207   D. 130

3. Of the following meters, the one which MOST probably should have been reported in the column OTHER UNUSUAL CONDITION is

   A. 110   B. 166   C. 189   D. 221

4. Of the following meters, the one which MOST probably should NOT have been reported in the column COIN BOX MISSING is

   A. 135   B. 140   C. 166   D. 176

5. Of the following meters, the one which MOST probably should NOT have been reported in the column OTHER UNUSUAL CONDITION is

   A. 168   B. 173   C. 177   D. 206

6. Of the following meters, the one which MOST probably was reported in the CORRECT column is

   A. 117   B. 153   C. 194   D. 202

7. Of the following meters, the one which MOST probably was reported in the WRONG column is

   A. 145   B. 161   C. 167   D. 181

8. Of the following meters, the one which MOST probably was reported in the CORRECT column is

   A. 102   B. 117   C. 148   D. 210

9. Of the following meters, the one which MOST probably was reported in the WRONG column is

   A. 123   B. 140   C. 202   D. 230

10. Of the following meters, the one which MOST probably has been INCOMPLETELY reported is

    A. 123   B. 176   C. 177   D. 216

KEY (CORRECT ANSWERS)

1. C
2. C
3. D
4. A
5. D

6. C
7. A
8. C
9. C
10. A

TEST 3

Questions 1-10.

DIRECTIONS: Questions 1 through 10 are to be answered SOLELY on the basis of the information given in the table below.

PARKING METER COLLECTIONS - CITY A

Zone	Meter No.	Jan.	Feb.	Mar.	Apr.	Total
ZONE W	1063	$ 76.35	$ 89.30	$ 77.14	$ 86.16	$ 328.95
	1064	49.72	56.61	63.29	73.29	242.91
	1065	73.15	52.79	88.17	84.17	298.28
	1066	80.62	74.73	54.69	23.61	233.65
	TOTAL	$279.84	$273.43	$283.29	$267.23	$1,103.79
ZONE X	769	$ 60.29	$ 50.27	$ 62.73	$ 76.53	$ 249.82
	770	81.40	73.12	70.51	40.27	265.30
	771	72.49	77.86	61.26	79.51	291.12
	772	65.14	62.40	70.91	72.26	270.71
	TOTAL	$279.32	$263.65	$265.41	$268.57	$1,076.95
ZONE Y	815	$ 61.67	$ 60.96	$ 73.71	$ 68.92	$ 265.26
	816	41.92	44.63	46.17	47.74	180.46
	817	78.72	60.73	63.55	72.78	275.78
	TOTAL	$182.31	$166.32	$183.43	$189.44	$ 721.50
ZONE Z	963	$ 59.36	$ 63.53	$ 76.35	76.35	$ 275.59
	964	42.53	40.13	58.36	66.72	207.74
	965	77.72	63.27	70.37	80.15	291.51
	966	56.87	60.46	74.53	72.62	264.48
	967	62.35	59.50	60.29	59.62	241.76
	TOTAL	$298.83	$286.89	$339.90	$355.46	$1,281.08

1. The parking meter zone which, on the average, collected MOST per meter for the four-month period is Zone

   A. W   B. X   C. Y   D. Z

2. The 2 months in which the total collections in Zone X was MORE than 1 1/2 times but LESS than 2 times the total collections in Zone Y are _____ and _____.

   A. January; February   B. January; March
   C. February; March   D. March; April

3. In March, there was more money collected than in February but less than in April in each zone EXCEPT Zone

   A. W   B. X   C. Y   D. Z

4. Parking meter number 770 was known to be out of order during part of one month. Judging only by the amount of collections, it is MOST likely that the month in which it was out of order is

   A. January   B. February   C. March   D. April

5. The greatest INCREASE in one month's total collections over the previous month occurred in Zone

   A. W   B. X   C. Y   D. Z

6. The greatest DECREASE in one month's total collections over the previous month occurred in Zone

   A. W   B. X   C. Y   D. Z

7. The month in which more than $175 but less than $300 was collected in each zone is

   A. January   B. February   C. March   D. April

8. The 2 parking meters which showed a steady monthly INCREASE in collections from January through April are _____ and _____.

   A. 963; 1064
   B. 1064; 816
   C. 966; 816
   D. 966; 1064

9. The 2 parking meters which showed a steady monthly DECREASE in collections from January through April are _____ and _____.

   A. 1066; 770
   B. 770; 967
   C. 1066; 967
   D. 770; 964

10. The parking meter from which the amount of money collected remained MOST NEARLY the same from month to month is

    A. 771   B. 967   C. 1063   D. 815

KEY (CORRECT ANSWERS)

1. A
2. A
3. A
4. D
5. D

6. A
7. A
8. B
9. A
10. B

TEST 4

Questions 1-5.

DIRECTIONS: Questions 1 through 5 are to be answered SOLELY on the basis of the information given in the following chart.

```
                    COLLECTION DIVISION
                    PARKING METER FIELD
                    OPERATION REPORT

                                           Date: Jan. 4
```

Location	Time Arrived	Time Departed	Elapsed Time	
			Travel	Collection
Office		9:15	Hr. Min.	Hr. Min.
2407	10:00	10:35	45	35
3502	10:45	11:15	10	30
2574	11:20	12:50	5	1 30
Lunch	1:05	2:05	15	
3379	2:05	2:55		50
2810	3:05	3:30	10	25
3208	3:35	4:00	5	25
Office	4:45		45	
		Total		

Remarks: _____

Mileage Start	174		Vehicle No.	12
Close	209		Total Crew	3
Daily Total	35			

Parking Meter Areas Assigned: 2407, 3502, 2574, 3379, 2810, 3208

James Roe
Driver

1. According to the information in the report and assuming equal traffic conditions, which of the following statements about the distances between locations is TRUE?

    A. If the crew car was always driven at an average speed of 25 miles an hour, the crew never travelled less than 2 miles to get from one location to another.
    B. The last location the crew worked at was farther from the office than the first location they worked at.
    C. The place where the crew ate lunch was right near the last place they worked at before lunch.
    D. Travelling from one assigned parking meter area to the next, the crew never travelled as far as when they went from the first to the second location they worked at.

1.___

2. Which of the following items of information can be obtained from the report? 2._____

   A. Average time spent collecting at each location
   B. The license of the vehicle
   C. When the crew got to the office in the morning
   D. When the crew left the office in the afternoon

3. Suppose that, on the average, the same amount of time was spent by a parking meter collector in collecting from any meter. 3._____
   Therefore, according to the report, the parking meter area that had approximately 1/3 as many meters as Area 2574 is

   A. 2407   B. 3502   C. 3379   D. 2810

4. Information which CANNOT be obtained from this report alone is the 4._____

   A. distance travelled
   B. total time spent collecting
   C. number of meters collected from
   D. total time spent travelling

5. Judging from the information in the report, it is MOST probable that 5._____

   A. members of the crew took turns driving
   B. nothing unusual happened to this crew that day
   C. the crew did not take their full time for lunch
   D. the crew was made up of a driver and a collector

KEY (CORRECT ANSWERS)

1. A
2. A
3. B
4. C
5. B

TEST 5

Questions 1-6.

DIRECTIONS: Questions 1 through 6 are to be answered SOLELY on the basis of the information given in the table below.

RIVER CITY - WEEKLY REPORT - WEEK ENDING 7/17				
	No. of Parking Meters		No. of Summonses Issued	
	On Streets	In Parking Lots	Overtime Parking	Other Violations
Zone P	840	1,680	460	130
Zone Q	1,400	420	1,200	480
Zone R	920	460	520	180
Zone S	1,550	620	800	200
Zone T	750	2,250	400	120

1. Compared to the total number of parking meters On *Streets*, the TOTAL number of parking meters *In Parking Lots* is

   A. 30 less   B. 60 less   C. 90 more   D. 30 more

2. Of all the summonses given out in Zone S during the week, what percent were for *Other Violations*?

   A. 25%   B. 20%   C. 15%   D. 5%

3. The average number of summonses issued for overtime parking in each Zone during the week is MOST NEARLY

   A. 225   B. 340   C. 675   D. 1,090

4. Suppose that an employee can check 40 meters an hour on the streets and 3 times that number in a parking lot. If an employee works 7 hours a day, excluding a lunch period, and each meter is checked twice- a day, how many employees must be assigned daily to Zone P to check all the meters?

   A. 7   B. 8   C. 10   D. 12

5. Suppose that a new parking lot is to be built in Zone Q. How many metered spaces must there be in this new parking lot so that Zone Q will have the same ratio of street meters to parking lot meters as Zone R?

   A. 700   B. 440   C. 350   D. 280

6. Comparing the total number of parking meters with the total number of summonses issued, it is CORRECT to state that the zone with the _____ number of meters issued the _____ number of summonses.

   A. smallest; smallest
   C. smallest; largest
   B. largest; largest
   D. largest; smallest

KEY (CORRECT ANSWERS)

1. A
2. B
3. C
4. C
5. D
6. D

READING COMPREHENSION
UNDERSTANDING AND INTERPRETING WRITTEN MATERIAL

EXAMINATION SECTION
TEST 1

DIRECTIONS: Each question or incomplete statement is followed by several suggested answers or completions. Select the one that BEST answers the question or completes the statement. *PRINT THE LETTER OF THE CORRECT ANSWER IN THE SPACE AT THE RIGHT.*

Questions 1-4.

DIRECTIONS: Questions 1 through 4 are to be answered SOLELY on the basis of the following paragraph.

When a vehicle has been disabled in the tunnel, the officer on patrol in this zone shall press the emergency truck light button. In the fast lane, red lights will go on throughout the tunnel; in the slow lane, amber lights will go on throughout the tunnel. The yellow zone light will go on at each signal control station throughout the tunnel and will flash the number of the zone in which the stoppage has occurred. A red flashing pilot light will appear only at the signal control station at which the emergency truck button was pressed. The emergency garage will receive an audible and visual signal indicating the signal control station at which the emergency truck button was pressed. The garage officer shall acknowledge receipt of the signal by pressing the acknowledgment button. This will cause the pilot light at the operated signal control station in the tunnel to cease flashing and to remain steady. It is an answer to the officer at the operated signal control station that the emergency truck is responding to the call.

1. According to this paragraph, when the emergency truck light button is pressed, 1.____

    A. amber lights will go on in every lane throughout the tunnel
    B. emergency signal lights will go on only in the lane in which the disabled vehicle happens to be
    C. red lights will go on in the fast lane throughout the tunnel
    D. pilot lights at all signal control stations will turn amber

2. According to this paragraph, the number of the zone in which the stoppage has occurred is flashed 2.____

    A. immediately after all the lights in the tunnel turn red
    B. by the yellow zone light at each signal control station
    C. by the emergency truck at the point of stoppage
    D. by the emergency garage

3. According to this paragraph, an officer near the disabled vehicle will know that the emergency tow truck is coming when 3.____

    A. the pilot light at the operated signal control station appears and flashes red
    B. an audible signal is heard in the tunnel

77

C. the zone light at the operated signal control station turns red
D. the pilot light at the operated signal control station becomes steady

4. Under the system described in the paragraph, it would be CORRECT to come to the conclusion that

   A. officers at all signal control stations are expected to acknowledge that they have received the stoppage signal
   B. officers at all signal control stations will know where the stoppage has occurred
   C. all traffic in both lanes of that side of the tunnel in which the stoppage has occurred must stop until the emergency truck has arrived
   D. there are two emergency garages, each able to respond to stoppages in traffic going in one particular direction

Questions 5-8.

DIRECTIONS: Questions 5 through 8 are to be answered SOLELY on the basis of the information given in the paragraph below.

A summons is an official statement ordering a person to appear in court. In traffic violation situations, summonses are used when arrests need not be made. The main reason for traffic summonses is to deter motorists from repeating the same traffic violation. Occasionally, motorists may make unintentional driving errors, and sometimes they are unaware of correct driving regulations. In cases such as these, the policy should be to have the officer verbally inform the motorist of the violation and warn him against repeating it. The purpose of this practice is not to limit the number of summonses, but rather to prevent the issuing of summonses when the violation is not due to deliberate intent or to inexcusable negligence.

5. According to the above paragraph, the PRINCIPAL reason for issuing traffic summonses is to

   A. discourage motorists from violating these laws again
   B. increase the money collected by the city
   C. put traffic violators in prison
   D. have them serve as substitutes for police officers

6. The reason a verbal warning may sometimes be substituted for a summons is to

   A. limit the number of summonses
   B. distinguish between excusable and inexcusable violations
   C. provide harsher penalties for deliberate intent than for inexcusable negligence
   D. decrease the caseload in the courts

7. The above paragraph implies that someone who violated a traffic regulation because he did NOT know about the regulation should be

   A. put under arrest   B. fined less money
   C. given a summons   D. told not to do it again

8. Using the distinctions made by the above paragraph, the one of the following motorists to whom it would be MOST desirable to issue a summons is the one who exceeded the speed limit because he

   A. did not know the speed limit
   B. was late for an important business appointment
   C. speeded to avoid being hit by another car
   D. had a speedometer which was not working properly

Questions 9-11.

DIRECTIONS: Questions 9 through 11 are to be answered in accordance with the paragraphs below.

The proper use of artificial respiration is of the greatest importance when breathing has stopped in cases of electric shock, gas poisoning, or drowning.

The first minutes in applying artificial respiration are most important. It should start immediately and be continued without interruption (if necessary for four hours) until natural breathing is restored. Someone else should call the doctor.

The first step in cases of electric shock is to instantly break the contact. Any available non-conductor can be used for this purpose, but the hands of the individual applying artificial respiration must be protected to avoid further accident (if possible, shut off the current or break the circuit).

The victim of gas poisoning must immediately receive fresh air, preferably in a warm dry atmosphere. Use proper protective equipment before entering gas-filled atmosphere. If such equipment is not available, hold your breath while you dash in and drag out the victim.

9. In cases of electric shock, the FIRST step to take is to

   A. lay the victim face down and start artificial respiration
   B. give the victim a stimulant
   C. break the contact with the live circuit
   D. put a blanket over the victim

10. In cases of gas poisoning, the FIRST step to take is to

    A. lay the victim face down and take foreign objects out of his mouth
    B. give the victim a stimulant
    C. cover the victim with blankets
    D. take the victim out of the gas-filled atmosphere and into the fresh air

11. Artificial respiration should be continued

    A. for half an hour *only*
    B. for two or three hours *only*
    C. until the victim"s face becomes flushed
    D. until the victim's natural breathing is restored or a physician tells you to stop

Questions 12-15.

DIRECTIONS: Questions 12 through 15 are to be answered in accordance with the paragraphs below.

Lay the victim face down, with one arm extended directly overhead, the other arm bent at the elbow with his face turned outward resting on hand or forearm to keep nose and mouth free for breathing. Kneel straddling the victim's hips with the knees just below the patient's hip bones. Place your palms on the small of his back, with fingers on ribs, little finger just touching the lowest rib. This is important as placing fingers too high may cause a rib injury; placing them too low puts pressure on kidneys where it does no good and may do harm.

Swing forward gradually bringing your weight to bear. Keep arms stiff. Shoulders should be directly over back of hand. After about two seconds, release pressure gradually by swinging back on your heels and letting hands drop. Repeat this sequence of operations smoothly and rhythmically.

While you continue artificial respiration, any helpers you may have should take any foreign objects (if any) out of the victim's mouth, cover him with blankets or coats, and send for a doctor immediately.

12. In applying artificial respiration, you should kneel straddling the victim with your knees

    A. just below the shoulders
    B. halfway between the small of the back and the shoulders
    C. midway between the mid-point of the thighs and the knees
    D. just below the hip bones

13. One of the MOST important reasons why the hands should not be placed too low in applying artificial respiration is that this

    A. may result in a broken rib
    B. may injure the liver
    C. does no good
    D. is likely to cause the victim to inhale when he should exhale

14. In applying artificial respiration, you should swing forward

    A. quickly with arms stiff
    B. quickly with arms bent
    C. gradually with arms bent
    D. gradually with arms stiff

15. While you are giving artificial respiration, your assistants should

    A. give the victim a stimulant and cover him with blankets immediately
    B. take foreign objects out of the victim's mouth and give him a stimulant immediately
    C. dash water in his face and give him a drink of water immediately
    D. take foreign objects out of his mouth and send for a doctor immediately

Questions 16-23.

DIRECTIONS: Questions 16 through 23 are to be answered ONLY on the basis of the Rules for Bridge and Tunnel Officers given below.

RULES FOR BRIDGE AND TUNNEL OFFICERS

I. Officers shall give their name, rank, and badge number to any person who requests it.
II. An officer on duty at a tunnel post shall immediately press the button for fire, obstructed lane, or dangerous vehicle when one of these conditions exist.
III. If the driver of a vehicle does not have the cash or stamped ticket to pay a toll, he shall not be allowed to use the facility.
IV. An officer shall permit only authorized persons on official business to be in a toll booth or at a tunnel post.
V. An officer in a toll booth shall get assistance from his supervisor in any situation when he is unsure whether a vehicle should be allowed to proceed.

16. An officer collects the correct toll from a truck driver. However, the driver says that bridge tolls are too high and in an angry voice asks the officer for his name and number so that he can write a letter about the high tolls. Of the following, the BEST thing for the officer to do is to

   A. tell the driver that he is holding up traffic and should move on
   B. give his name and badge number to the driver
   C. tell the driver not to use the bridge anymore if the toll is too high
   D. provide the driver with reasons for the tolls charged

17. While on duty at a post in a tunnel, an officer notices a driver putting out a small fire in the engine of a car. At that moment, the driver turns to the officer and yells, *I can put it out myself.* The FIRST thing the officer should do is

   A. help the driver put out the fire
   B. press the button which signals a fire in the tunnel
   C. let the motorist handle the situation himself
   D. call his supervisor and ask for help

18. A motorist approaching a bridge stops at a toll booth and hands the officer postage stamps instead of coins to pay the toll.
The officer should FIRST

   A. refuse the stamps and tell the driver that the bridge toll must be paid in cash
   B. accept the stamps as payment of the toll
   C. request assistance in dealing with the situation
   D. refuse the stamps, let the vehicle go on, but have the driver promise that he will return with the money

19. An officer at a post inside a tunnel sees two large cartons fall off a truck.
The officer's FIRST response should be to

   A. try to move the cartons to the side of the roadway
   B. signal another officer to stop the truck at the tunnel's exit
   C. run after the truck to tell the driver what has happened
   D. use an appropriate signal button

20. Suppose that, while an officer is collecting tolls, a car stops at the toll booth and the driver appears to be drunk.
Of the following, the FIRST thing the officer should do is to

   A. tell the driver to proceed very carefully and be sure not to drive after drinking in the future
   B. signal another officer to assist him in escorting the driver to their supervisor
   C. refuse to accept the toll money and call his supervisor
   D. immediately press the emergency button

21. While on duty inside a tunnel, an officer notices that a car has stopped and has a flat tire. It is late evening, and there is no other traffic visible.
The FIRST thing the officer should do is to

   A. quickly assist the driver in changing the tire
   B. signal that a lane is blocked
   C. tell the driver to drive out of the tunnel
   D. issue a summons to the motorist for stopping his car inside a tunnel

22. Suppose that a friend tells an officer that he is interested in learning about the officer's work. The friend says that he would like to visit the officer in a toll booth for an hour the next day.
Of the following, which one is the BEST reply for the officer to make?

   A. Sorry, but I'm not allowed to let you in the booth.
   B. You can stay in the booth, but be careful not to touch anything
   C. You can't come inside the booth, but you can stay with me in the tunnel.
   D. It's all right, but be sure to give my name, rank, and number if anyone questions you.

23. Assume that, while an officer is collecting a toll from a motorist, the officer sees a child tied up in the rear of the car.
Of the following, the BEST thing for the officer to do is to

   A. ignore what he has seen and continue collecting tolls
   B. try to delay the car and signal for assistance
   C. reach into the car and untie the child
   D. tell the driver that he cannot use the bridge unless he unties the child

Questions 24-30.

DIRECTIONS: Questions 24 through 30 are to be answered SOLELY on the basis of the information contained in the following paragraphs.

Snow-covered roads spell trouble for motorists all winter long. Clearing highways of snow and ice to keep millions of motor vehicles moving freely is a tremendous task. Highway departments now rely, to a great extent, on chemical deicers to get the big job done. Sodium chloride, in the form of commercial salt, is the deicer most frequently used.

There is no reliable evidence to prove that salt reduces highway accidents. But available statistics are impressive. For example, before Massachusetts used chemical deicers, it had a yearly average of 21 fatal accidents and 1,635 injuries attributed to cars skidding on snow or ice. Beginning in 1940, the state began fighting hazardous driving conditions with chemical deicers. During the period 1940-50, there was a yearly average of only seven deaths and 736 injuries as a result of skids.

Economical and effective in a moderately low temperature range, salt is increasingly popular with highway departments, but not so A popular with individual car owners. Salty slush eats away at metal, including auto bodies. It also sprinkles windshields with a fine-grained spray which dries on contact, severely reducing visibility. However, drivers who are hindered or immobilized by heavy winter weather favor the liberal use of products such as sodium chloride. When snow blankets roads, these drivers feel that the quickest way to get back to the safety of driving on bare pavement is through use of deicing salts.

24. The MAIN reason given by the above passage for the use of sodium chloride as a deicer is that it

    A. has no harmful side effects
    B. is economical
    C. is popular among car owners
    D. reduces highway accidents

25. The above passage may BEST be described as a(n)

    A. argument against the use of sodium chloride as a deicer
    B. discussion of some advantages and disadvantages of sodium chloride as a deicer
    C. recommendation to use sodium chloride as a deicer
    D. technical account of the uses and effects of sodium chloride as a deicer

26. Based on the above passage, the use of salt on snow-covered roadways will EVENTUALLY

    A. decrease the efficiency of the automotive fuel
    B. cause tires to deteriorate
    C. damage the surface of the roadway
    D. cause holes in the sides of cars

27. The AVERAGE number of persons killed yearly in Massachusetts in car accidents caused by skidding on snow or ice before chemical deicers were used there was

    A. 9   B. 12   C. 21   D. 30

28. According to the passage, it would be ADVISABLE to use salt as a deicer when

    A. outdoor temperatures are somewhat below freezing
    B. residues on highway surfaces are deemed to be undesirable
    C. snow and ice have low absorbency characteristics
    D. the use of a substance is desired which dries on contact

29. As a result of using chemical deicers, the number of injuries resulting from skids in Massachusetts was reduced by about

    A. 35%   B. 45%   C. 55%   D. 65%

30. According to the above passage, driver visibility can be severely reduced by

    A. sodium chloride deposits on the windshield
    B. glare from salt and snow crystals
    C. salt spray covering the front lights
    D. faulty windshield wipers

KEY (CORRECT ANSWERS)

1.	C	16.	B
2.	B	17.	B
3.	D	18.	A
4.	B	19.	D
5.	A	20.	C
6.	B	21.	B
7.	D	22.	A
8.	B	23.	B
9.	C	24.	B
10.	D	25.	B
11.	D	26.	D
12.	D	27.	C
13.	C	28.	A
14.	D	29.	C
15.	D	30.	A

TEST 2

DIRECTIONS: Each question or incomplete statement is followed by several suggested answers or completions. Select the one that BEST answers the question or completes the statement. *PRINT THE LETTER OF THE CORRECT ANSWER IN THE SPACE AT THE RIGHT.*

Questions 1-3.

DIRECTIONS: Questions 1 through 3 are to be answered according to the information contained in the following paragraph.

Each parking meter collector shall keep a permanently-bound notebook record of each day's field activities, noting therein the date, area, and the numbers of the meters from which collections were made or which were serviced by him. While at the meter, he shall also note therein any reason why a coin box was not collected or bulk revenue was not collected; the number and denominations of all loose coins found in the coin compartment of a coin box meter; those meters which are damaged in any respect and the nature of such damage; why a meter was not placed in operation; and any other information or circumstance which may affect the collections, revenue, operation or maintenance of the meters he serviced. Any damage to collection equipment and the nature of the damage shall also be noted in such book. All such notations shall be set forth on the prescribed daily report form to be made out by the employee at the conclusion of each day's assignment. Said report shall be signed by all of the members of the collection crew.

1. The term *bulk revenue* in the above passage MOST probably refers to   1._____

    A. money not in a coin box
    B. money in a coin box
    C. money not taken from a meter
    D. paper money

2. A parking meter collector finds 60¢ in loose coins (3 nickels, 2 dimes, 1 quarter) in the coin compartment of a coin box meter.   2._____
Of the following, the BEST way to enter this in his notebook is *loose coins*

    A. 60¢
    B. 2 dimes, 3 nickels, 1 quarter
    C. 6, 60? total
    D. 3 Jefferson nickels, 2 Roosevelt dimes, 1 Washington quarter

3. The parking meter collector's daily report form is MAINLY intended to be used to report the   3._____

    A. activities of collection crews with more than one or two members
    B. information not recorded in the bound notebook
    C. information recorded in the bound notebook
    D. unusual occurrences of the day

Questions 4-12.

DIRECTIONS: Questions 4 through 12 are to be answered according to the rules listed below.

RULES FOR BRIDGE OPERATION

When a vessel owned by the U.S. Government or the city approaches a movable bridge, it shall signal with four *distinct* blasts of a whistle.

All other vessels signal with three distinct blasts of a whistle.

All call signals for openings shall be answered promptly by the bridge by 2 long distinct blasts.
This signal indicates to the boat that the call signal has been heard, and preparations to open will be made.

After this signal, the Bridge Operator shall open his bridge at such a time which in his judgment and experience will permit *prompt* passage of the boat without unreasonable delay and will not create any unreasonable delay to land traffic.

At no time shall the draw be moved until all sidewalk and roadway traffic gates are locked in their closed position.

If the draw cannot be opened, the 2 blast signal shall be repeated until acknowledged by the boat.

It is *extremely* important that the draw be brought to its fully opened position at all times, irrespective of the size of the boat. (This does not apply to test openings.)

When the draw is fully opened, the Bridge Operator shall sound the same signal as the call signal.

While the draw is in its fully opened position, no attempt shall be made toward closing until the passing boat has cleared the draw.

Except in rare emergencies, the draw shall not be moved either in closing or opening while there is a boat in the draw.

When the draw is fully closed and land traffic can be resumed, the Bridge Operator is to sound one blast which will be the signal for the Bridge Tenders to open all traffic gates.

Visual signals shall be used as prescribed by the Department of the Army whenever sound signals cannot be given or if sound signals cannot be heard.

The time of an opening shall be the *interval* between the time the traffic gates are closed and the time they are opened.

4. As used above, *prompt* means MOST NEARLY
   A. easy B. safe C. speedy D. careful

5. As used above, *extremely* means MOST NEARLY
   A. very B. mildly C. of course D. sometimes

6. As used above, *visual* means MOST NEARLY
   A. telegraph B. bell C. runner D. sight

7. According to the above statements, if an approaching vessel signals for an opening with 4 blasts, it means that the vessel is
   A. a tanker
   B. a tug
   C. foreign-owned
   D. city-owned

8. According to the above rules, a boat approaching a bridge will signal the bridge by
   A. swinging a red light
   B. calling through a megaphone
   C. blowing a whistle
   D. waving a blue flag

9. According to the above rules, the bridge answers the boat by blowing a whistle
   A. once
   B. twice
   C. three times
   D. four times

10. According to the above rules, when a bridge is opened for passage of a boat, the amount that the bridge is opened will
    A. vary, depending on the size of boat *only*
    B. vary, depending on the tide *only*
    C. vary, depending on the size of boat and the tide
    D. always be the same

11. According to the above rules, the operator NORMALLY will begin to close the bridge
    A. as soon as the boat enters the draw, so the operator knows the height of the boat
    B. when the center of the boat has passed the center of the bridge
    C. at any time convenient to the operator
    D. after the boat has completely passed through the draw

12. According to the above rules, the man operating the traffic gate knows the bridge is closed when he
    A. sees the bridge operator wave
    B. sees the traffic signals turn green
    C. feels the bridge come together
    D. hears a single blast on a whistle

Questions 13-16.

DIRECTIONS: Questions 13 through 16 are to be answered according to the information contained in the following paragraph.

When reporting for work each day, an assistant bridge operator is required to sign his time card. At this time, he will read the notices published on the bulletin board for any changes in rules or special conditions that may affect him. After changing into work clothes, the supervisor will assign the assistant bridge operator to any work that has to be done. When the bridge is not open, there may be tasks such as cleaning the motor room, oiling the machinery-or minor repair work. When the bridge is to be opened, the assistant bridge operator will go to his post at one end of the bridge and will signal all traffic to stop by means of lights. Immediately thereafter, he will start to lower the barricades. However, the barricades will not be completely lowered until all traffic has stopped. The bridge is then opened.

13. According to the above paragraph, the FIRST thing an assistant bridge operator does when reporting for work is to

    A. read the bulletin board
    B. change to work clothes
    C. sign his time card
    D. report to his supervisor

14. The purpose of reading the bulletin board is to

    A. find out what work has to be done
    B. see who the supervisor is
    C. save time
    D. be aware of any changes in rules

15. Work to which the assistant bridge operator may be assigned is

    A. oiling the motors
    B. hand signalling traffic
    C. replacing the lift cables
    D. opening the bridge

16. Lowering of the barricades is begun

    A. before signalling the traffic to stop
    B. at the same time as the traffic is signalled to stop
    C. immediately after the traffic is signalled to stop
    D. after all traffic has stopped

Questions 17-30.

DIRECTIONS: Questions 17 through 30 are to be answered according to your memory of the information contained in the paragraph below.

At 8:30 A.M. on Friday, February 2, Assistant Bridge Operator Henry Jones started to clean the walk of the Avenue X Bridge. It was snowing heavily, and the surface of the road was slippery. At 8:32 A.M., Mr. Jones saw a westbound station wagon skid and strike a westbound sedan about 50 feet from the barrier. Both cars were badly damaged. The station wagon was overturned and came to rest 8 feet from the barrier. The woman driver of the station wagon, Mrs. Harriet White, was thrown clear and landed in the middle of the road. The other car was smashed against the barrier. The driver of the sedan, Mr. Tom Green, was pinned behind the steering wheel and suffered cuts about the face. Mr. Jones called the Bridge Operator, Mr. Frank Smith, who telephoned for an ambulance. First aid was given to both drivers. They were taken to the Avenue W Hospital by an ambulance which was driven by Mr. James Doe and arrived on the scene at 9:07 A.M. Patrolman John Brown, Badge No. 71162, had arrived before the ambulance and recorded all the details of the accident, including the statements of Mr. Henry Jones and of Mr. Jack Black, another eyewitness.

17. The accident occurred on

    A. Saturday, February 3
    B. Saturday, February 2
    C. Friday, February 2
    D. Friday, February 3

18. The time of the accident was

    A. 7:32 A.M.   B. 8:32 A.M.
    C. 8:32 P.M.   D. 7:32 P.M.

19. The Assistant Bridge Operator's name was

    A. Frank Smith   B. Tom Jones
    C. Henry Smith   D. Henry Jones

20. The accident involved a _____ and _____.

    A. sedan; a station wagon
    B. station wagon; a panel truck
    C. station wagon; two sedans
    D. sedan; two station wagons

21. The man named Jack Black was a(n)

    A. patrolman   B. eyewitness
    C. ambulance driver   D. street cleaner

22. The time which elapsed between the accident and the arrival of the ambulance was MOST NEARLY _____ minutes.

    A. 7   B. 28   C. 32   D. 35

23. The weather was

    A. fair   B. rainy   C. sleety   D. snowy

24. The station wagon was driven by

    A. Jane Brown   B. Jane White
    C. Harriet White   D. Harriet Brown

25. Tom Green was the

    A. driver of the ambulance
    B. driver of the sedan
    C. other eyewitness
    D. patrolman

26. The barrier was

    A. struck by the sedan
    B. struck by the station wagon
    C. struck by both cars
    D. not struck by either car

27. The damage done to

    A. both cars was slight
    B. the sedan was severe but that done to the station wagon was slight
    C. the station wagon was severe but that done to the sedan was slight
    D. both cars was severe

28. The woman driver

    A. was pinned behind the wheel
    B. suffered face cuts
    C. was thrown clear
    D. was trapped in the car

29. The name of the Bridge Operator was

    A. Frank Smith   B. John Smith
    C. Henry Jones   D. Frank Jones

30. When the accident occurred, the _____ feet from the barrier.

    A. station wagon was 20   B. cars were 50
    C. sedan was 60   D. sedan was 8

KEY (CORRECT ANSWERS)

1.	A	16.	C
2.	B	17.	C
3.	C	18.	B
4.	C	19.	D
5.	A	20.	A
6.	D	21.	B
7.	D	22.	D
8.	C	23.	D
9.	B	24.	C
10.	D	25.	B
11.	D	26.	A
12.	D	27.	D
13.	C	28.	C
14.	D	29.	A
15.	A	30.	B

CODING

EXAMINATION SECTION

COMMENTARY

An ingenious question-type called coding, involving elements of alphabetizing, filing, name and number comparison, and evaluative judgment and application, has currently won wide acceptance in testing circles for measuring clerical aptitude and general ability, particularly on the senior (middle) grades (levels).

While the directions for this question usually vary in detail, the candidate is generally asked to consider groups of names, codes, and numbers, and then, according to a given plan, to arrange codes in alphabetic order; to arrange these in numerical sequence; to re-arrange columns of names and numbers in correct order; to espy errors in coding; to choose the correct coding arrangement in consonance with the given directions and examples, etc.

This question-type appear to have few parameters in respect to form, substance, or degree of difficulty.

Accordingly, acquaintance with, and practice in, the coding question is recommended for the serious candidate.

TEST 1

DIRECTIONS: Questions 1 through 8 are to be answered on the basis of the code table and the instructions given below.

Code Letter for Traffic Problem	B	H	Q	J	F	L	M	I
Code Number for Action Taken	1	2	3	4	5	6	7	8

Assume that each of the capital letters on the above chart is a radio code for a particular traffic problem and that the number immediately below each capital letter is the radio code for the correct action to be taken to deal with the problem. For instance, "1" is the action to be taken to deal with problem "B", "2" is the action to be taken to deal with problem "H", and so forth.

In each question, a series of code letters is given in Column 1. Column 2 gives four different arrangements of code numbers. You are to pick the answer (A, B, C, or D) in Column 2 that gives the code numbers that match the code letters in the same order.

SAMPLE QUESTION

Column 1
BHLFMQ

Column 2
A. 125678
B. 216573
C. 127653
D. 126573

According to the chart, the code numbers that correspond to these code letters are as follows: B – 1, M – 2, L – 6, F – 5, M – 7, Q – 3. Therefore, the right answer is 126573. This answer is D in Column 2.

2 (#1)

	Column 1	Column 2	

1. BHQLMI
   - A. 123456
   - B. 123567
   - C. 123678
   - D. 125678

   1.____

2. HBJQLF
   - A. 214365
   - B. 213456
   - C. 213465
   - D. 214387

   2.____

3. QHMLFJ
   - A. 321654
   - B. 345678
   - C. 327645
   - D. 327654

   3.____

4. FLQJIM
   - A. 543287
   - B. 563487
   - C. 564378
   - D. 654378

   4.____

5. FBIHMJ
   - A. 518274
   - B. 152874
   - C. 528164
   - D. 517842

   5.____

6. MIHFQB
   - A. 872341
   - B. 782531
   - C. 782341
   - D. 783214

   6.____

7. JLFHQIM
   - A. 465237
   - B. 456387
   - C. 4652387
   - D. 4562387

   7.____

8. LBJQIFH
   - A. 614382
   - B. 6134852
   - C. 61437852
   - D. 61431852

   8.____

KEY (CORRECT ANSWERS)

1.	C	5.	A
2.	A	6.	B
3.	D	7.	C
4.	B	8.	A

TEST 2

DIRECTIONS: Each question or incomplete statement is followed by several suggested answers or completions. Select the one that BEST answers the question or completes the statement. *PRINT THE LETTER OF THE CORRECT ANSWER IN THE SPACE AT THE RIGHT.*

Questions 1-5.

DIRECTIONS: Questions 1 through 5 are based on the following list showing the name and number of each of nine inmates.

1.	Johnson	4.	Thompson	7.	Gordon
2.	Smith	5.	Frank	8.	Porter
3.	Edwards	6.	Murray	9.	Lopez

Each question consists of 3 sets of numbers and letters. Each set should consist of the numbers of three inmates and the first letter of each of their names. The letters should be in the same order as the numbers. In at least two of the three choices, there will be an error. On your answer sheet, mark only that choice in which the letters correspond with the numbers and are in the same order. If all three sets are wrong, mark choice D in your answer space.

SAMPLE QUESTION
A. 386 EPM
B. 542 FST
C. 474 LGT

Since 3 corresponds to E for Edwards, 8 corresponds to P for Porter, and 6 corresponds to M for Murray, choice A is correct and should be entered in your answer space. Choice B is wrong because letters T and S have been reversed. Choice C is wrong because the first number, which is 4, does NOT correspond with the first letter of choice C, which is L. It should have been T. If choice A were also wrong, then D would be the correct answer.

1. A. 382 EGS   B. 461 TMJ   C. 875 PLF   1._____

2. A. 549 FLT   B. 692 MJS   C. 758 GSP   2._____

3. A. 936 LEM   B. 253 FSE   C. 147 JTL   3._____

4. A. 569 PML   B. 716 GJP   C. 842 PTS   4._____

5. A. 356 FEM   B. 198 JPL   C. 637 MEG   5._____

Questions 6-10.

DIRECTIONS: Questions 6 through 10 are to be answered on the basis of the following information:

2 (#3)

In order to make sure stock is properly located, incoming units are stored as follows:

STOCK NUMBERS	BIN NUMBERS
00100 – 39999	D30, L44
40000 – 69999	14L, D38
70000 – 99999	41L, 80D
100000 and over	614, 83D

Using the above table, choose the answer A, B, C, or D, which lists the correct Bin Number for the Stock Number given.

6. 17243
   A. 41L   B. 83D   C. 14L   D. D30

7. 9219
   A. D38   B. L44   C. 614   D. 41L

8. 90125
   A. 41L   B. 614   C. D38   D. D30

9. 10001
   A. L44   B. D38   C. 80D   D. 83D

10. 200100
   A. 41L   B. 14L   C. 83D   D. D30

KEY (CORRECT ANSWERS)

1.	B	6.	D
2.	D	7.	B
3.	A	8.	A
4.	C	9.	A
5.	C	10.	C

TEST 3

DIRECTIONS: Each question or incomplete statement is followed by several suggested answers or completions. Select the one that BEST answers the question or completes the statement. *PRINT THE LETTER OF THE CORRECT ANSWER IN THE SPACE AT THE RIGHT.*

Questions 1-9.

DIRECTIONS: Assume that the Police Department is planning to conduct a statistical study of individuals who have been convicted of crimes during a certain year. For the purpose of this study, identification numbers are being assigned to individuals in the following manner:

The first two digits indicate the age of the individual.
The third digit indicates the sex of the individual:
    1. Male
    2. Female
The fourth digit indicates the type of crime involved:
    1. criminal homicide
    2. forcible rape
    3. robbery
    4. aggravated assault
    5. burglary
    6. larceny
    7. auto theft
    8. other
The fifth and sixth digits indicate the month in which the conviction occurred:
    01.   January
    02.   February, etc.

Questions 1 through 9 are to be answered SOLELY on the basis of the above information and the following list of individuals and identification numbers.

Abbott, Richard	271304	Morris, Chris	212705
Collins, Terry	352111	Owens, William	231412
Elders, Edward	191207	Parker, Leonard	291807
George, Linda	182809	Robinson, Charles	311102
Hill, Leslie	251702	Sands, Jean	202610
Jones, Jackie	301106	Smith, Michael	42108
Lewis, Edith	402406	Turner, Donald	191601
Mack, Helen	332509	White, Barbara	242803

1. The number of women on the above list is   1.____
   A. 6   B. 7   C. 8   D. 9

2. The two convictions which occurred during February were for the crimes of
   A. aggravated assault and auto theft
   B. auto theft and criminal homicide
   C. burglary and larceny
   D. forcible rape and robbery

   2.____

3. The ONLY man convicted of auto theft was
   A. Richard Abbott   B. Leslie Hill
   C. Chris Morris   D. Leonard Parker

   3.____

4. The number of people on the list who were 25 years old or older is
   A. 6   B. 7   C. 8   D. 9

   4.____

5. The OLDEST person on the list is
   A. Terry Collins   B. Edith Lewis
   C. Helen Mack   D. Michael Smith

   5.____

6. The two people on the list who are the same age are
   A. Richard Abbott and Michael Smith
   B. Edward Elders and Donald Turner
   C. Linda George and Helen Mack
   D. Leslie Hill and Charles Robinson

   6.____

7. A 28-year-old man who was convicted of aggravated assault in October would have identification number
   A. 281410   B. 281509   C. 282311   D. 282409

   7.____

8. A 33-year-old woman convicted in April of criminal homicide would have identification number
   A. 331140   B. 331204   C. 332014   D. 332104

   8.____

9. The number of people on the above list who were convicted during the first six months of the year is
   A. 6   B. 7   C. 8   D. 9

   9.____

Questions 10-19.

DIRECTIONS: The following is a list of patients who were referred by various clinics to the laboratory for tests. After each name is a patient identification number. Questions 10 through 19 are to be answered on the basis of the information contained in this list and the explanation accompanying it.

The first digit refers to the clinic which made the referral:
1. cardiac
2. Renal
3. Pediatrics
4. Ophthalmology
5. Orthopedics
6. Hematology
7. Gynecology
8. Neurology
9. Gastroenterology

3 (#2)

The second digit refers to the sex of the patient:
1. male
2. female

The third and fourth digits give the age of the patient

The last two digits give the day of the month the laboratory tests were performed

LABORATORY REFERRALS DURING JANUARY

Adams, Jacqueline	320917	Miller, Michael	511806
Black, Leslie	813406	Pratt, William	214411
Cook, Marie	511616	Rogers, Ellen	722428
Fisher, Pat	914625	Saunders, Sally	310229
Jackson, Lee	923212	Wilson, Jan	416715
James, Linda	624621	Wyatt, Mark	321326
Lane, Arthur	115702		

10. According to the list, the number of women referred to the laboratory during January was
    A. 4   B. 5   C. 6   D. 7

11. The clinic from which the MOST patients were referred was
    A. Cardiac
    B. Gynecology
    C. Ophthalmology
    D. Pediatrics

12. The YOUNGEST patient referred from any clinic other than Pediatrics was
    A. Leslie Black
    B. Marie Cook
    C. Arthur Lane
    D. Sally Saunders

13. The number of patients whose laboratory tests were performed on or before January 16 was
    A. 7   B. 8   C. 9   D. 10

14. The number of patients referred for laboratory tests who are under age 45 is
    A. 7   B. 8   C. 9   D. 10

15. The OLDEST patient referred to the clinic during January was
    A. Jacqueline Adams
    B. Linda James
    C. Arthur Lane
    D. Jan Wilson

16. The ONLY patient treated in the Orthopedics clinic was
    A. Marie Cook
    B. Pat Fisher
    C. Ellen Rogers
    D. Jan Wilson

17. A woman, age 37 was referred from the Hematology clinic to the laboratory. Her laboratory tests were performed on January 9. Her identification number would be
    A. 610937   B. 623709   C. 613790   D. 623790

18. A man was referred for lab tests from the Orthopedics clinic. He is 30 years old 18.____
 and his tests were performed on January 6.
 His identification number would be
   A. 413006   B. 510360   C. 513006   D. 513060

19. A 4-year-old boy was referred from the Pediatrics clinic to have laboratory 19.____
 tests on January 23.
 His identification number was
   A. 310422   B. 310423   C. 310433   D. 320403

KEY (CORRECT ANSWERS)

1.	B	11.	D
2.	B	12.	B
3.	B	13.	A
4.	D	14.	C
5.	D	15.	D
6.	B	16.	A
7.	A	17.	B
8.	D	18.	C
9.	C	19.	B
10.	B		

TEST 4

DIRECTIONS: Each question or incomplete statement is followed by several suggested answers or completions. Select the one that BEST answers the question or completes the statement. *PRINT THE LETTER OF THE CORRECT ANSWER IN THE SPACE AT THE RIGHT.*

Questions 1-10.

DIRECTIONS: Questions 1 through 10 are to be answered on the basis of the information and directions given below.

Assume that you are a Senior Stenographer assigned to the personnel bureau of a city agency. Your supervisor has asked you to classify the employees in your agency into the following five groups:

- A. Employees who are college graduates, who are at least 35 years of age but less than 50, and who have been employed by the City for five years or more;
- B. Employees who have been employed by the City for less than five years, who are not college graduates, and who earn at least $32,500 a year but less than $34,500;
- C. Employees who have been City employees for five years or more, who are at least 21 years of age but less than 35, and who are not college graduates;
- D. Employee who earn at least $34,500 a year but less than $36,000 who are college graduates, and who have been employed by the City for less than five years;
- E. Employees who are not included in any of the foregoing groups.

NOTE: In classifying these employees you are to compute age and period of service as of January 1, 2003. In all cases, it is to be assumed that each employee has been employed continuously in City service. In each question, consider only the information which will assist you in classifying each employee Any information which is of no assistance in classifying an employee would not be considered.

SAMPLE: Mr. Brown, a 29-year-old veteran, was appointed to his present position of Clerk on June 1, 2000. He has completed two years of college. His present salary is $33,050.

The correct answer to this sample is B, since the employee has been employed by the City for less than five years, is not a college graduate, and earn at least $32,500 a year but less than $34,500.

Questions 1 through 10 contain excerpts from the personnel records of 10 employees in the agency. In the correspondingly numbered space at the right print the capital letter preceding the appropriate group into which you would place each employee.

1. Mr. James has been employed by the City since 1993, when he was graduated from a local college. Now 35 years of age, he earns $36,000 a year.   1._____

2. Mr. Worth began working in City service early in 1999. He was awarded his college degree in 1994, at the age of 21. As a result of a recent promotion, he now earns $34,500 a year.   2._____

2 (#4)

3. Miss Thomas has been a City employee since August 1, 1998. Her salary is $34,500 a year. Miss Thomas, who is 25 years old, has had only three years of high school training.

3._____

4. Mr. Williams has had three promotions since entering City service on January 1, 1991. He was graduated from college with honors in 1974, when he was 20 years of age. His present salary is $37,000 a year.

4._____

5. Miss Jones left college after two years of study to take an appointment to a position in the City service paying $33,300 a year. She began work on March 1, 1997 when she was 19 years of age.

5._____

6. Mr. Smith was graduated from an engineering college with honors in January 1998 and became a City employee three months later. His present salary is $35,810. Mr. Smith was born in 1976.

6._____

7. Miss Earnest was born on May 31, 1979. Her education consisted of four years of high school and one year of business school. She was appointed as a typist in a City agency on June 1, 1997. Her annual salary is $33,500.

7._____

8. Mr. Adams, a 24-year-old clerk, began his City service on July 1, 1999, soon after being discharged from the U.S. Army. A college graduate, his present annual salary is $33,200.

8._____

9. Miss Charles attends college in the evenings, hoping to obtain her degree is 2004, when she will be 30 years of age. She has been a City employee since April 1998, and earns $33,350.

9._____

10. Mr. Dolan was just promoted to his present position after six years of City service. He was graduated from high school in 1982, when he was 18 years of age, but did not go on to college. Mr. Dolan's present salary is $33,500.

10._____

KEY (CORRECT ANSWERS)

1.	A	6.	D
2.	D	7.	C
3.	E	8.	E
4.	A	9.	B
5.	C	10.	E

TEST 5

DIRECTIONS: Questions 1 through 4 each contain five numbers that should be arranged in numerical order. The number with the lowest numerical value should be first and the number with the highest numerical value should be last. Pick that option which indicates the CORRECT order of the numbers.

Examples: A. 9; 18; 14; 15; 27
           B. 9; 14; 15; 18; 27
           C. 14; 15; 18; 27; 9
           D. 9; 14; 15; 27; 18

The correct answer is B, which contains the proper arrangement of the five numbers.

1. A. 20573; 20753; 20738; 20837; 20098
   B. 20098; 20753; 20573; 20738; 20837
   C. 20098; 20573; 20753; 20837; 20738
   D. 20098; 20573; 20738; 20753; 20837

2. A. 113492; 113429; 111314; 113114; 131413
   B. 111314; 113114; 113429; 113492; 131413
   C. 111314; 113429; 113492; 113114; 131413
   D. 111314; 113114; 131413; 113429; 113492

3. A. 1029763; 1030421; 1035681; 1036928; 1067391
   B. 1030421; 1029763; 1035681; 1067391; 1036928
   C. 1030421; 1035681; 1036928; 1067391; 1029763
   D. 1029763; 1039421; 1035681; 1067391; 1036928

4. A. 1112315; 1112326; 1112337; 1112349; 1112306
   B. 1112306; 1112315; 1112337; 1112326; 1112349
   C. 1112306; 1112315; 1112326; 1112337; 1112349
   D. 1112306; 1112326; 1112315; 1112337; 1112349

KEY (CORRECT ANSWERS)

1. D
2. B
3. A
4. C

TEST 6

DIRECTIONS: The phonetic filing system is a method of filing names in which the alphabet is reduced to key code letters. The six key letters and their equivalents are as follows:

KEY LETTERS	EQUIVALENTS
b	p, f, v
c	s, k, g, j, q, x, z
d	t
l	none
m	n
r	none

A key letter represents itself.
Vowels (a, e, i, o, and u) and the letters w, h, and y are omitted.
For example, the name GILMAN would be represented as follows:
   G is represented by the key letter C.
   I is a vowel and is omitted.
   L is a letter and represents itself.
   M is a key letter and represents itself.
   A is a vowel and is omitted.
   N is represented by the key letter M.

Therefore, the phonetic filing code for the name GILMAN is CLMM.

Answer Questions 1 through 10 based on the information below.

1. The phonetic filing code for the name FITZGERALD would be
   A. BDCCRLD   B. BDCRLD   C. BDZCRLD   D. BTZCRLD

2. The phonetic filing code CLBR may represent any one of the following names EXCEPT
   A. Calprey   B. Flower   C. Glover   D. Silver

3. The phonetic filing code LDM may represent any one of the following names EXCEPT
   A. Halden   B. Hilton   C. Walton   D. Wilson

4. The phonetic filing code for the name RODRIGUEZ would be
   A. RDRC   B. RDRCC   C. RDRCZ   D. RTRCC

5. The phonetic filing code for the name MAXWELL would be
   A. MCLL   B. MCWL   C. MCWLL   D. MXLL

6. The phonetic filing code for the name ANDERSON would be
   A. AMDRCM   B. ENDRSM   C. MDRCM   D. NDERCN

7. The phonetic filing code for the name SAVITSKY would be
   A. CBDCC   B. CBDCY   C. SBDCC   D. SVDCC

8. The phonetic filing code CMC may represent any one of the following names EXCEPT
   A. James B. Jayes C. Johns D. Jones

9. The ONLY one of the following names that could be represented by the phonetic filing code CDDDM would be
   A. Catalano B. Chesterton C. Cittadino D. Cuttlerman

10. The ONLY one of the following names that could be represented by the phonetic filing code LLMCM would be
    A. Ellington B. Hallerman C. Inslerman D. Willingham

KEY (CORRECT ANSWERS)

1. A   6. C
2. B   7. A
3. D   8. B
4. B   9. C
5. A   10. D

NAME AND NUMBER CHECKING
EXAMINATION SECTION
TEST 1

DIRECTIONS: Questions 1 through 17 consist of sets of names and addresses. In each question, the name and address in Column II should be an exact copy of the name and address in Column I.
If there is:
a mistake only in the name, mark your answer A;
a mistake only in the address, mark your answer B;
a mistake in both name and address, mark your answer C;
No mistake in either name or address, mark your answer D.

Sample Question

Column I
Christina Magnusson
288 Greene Street
New York, N.Y. 10003

Column II
Christina Magnusson
288 Greene Street
New York, N.Y. 10013

Since there is a mistake only in the address (the zip code should be 10003 instead of 10013), the answer to the sample question is B.

COLUMN I

1. Ms. Joan Kelly
   313 Franklin Avenue
   Brooklyn, N.Y. 11202

2. Mrs. Eileen Engel
   47-24 86 Road
   Queens, N.Y. 11122

3. Marcia Michaels
   213 E. 81 St.
   New York, N.Y. 10012

4. Rev. Edward J. Smyth
   1401 Brandeis Street
   San Francisco, Calif. 96201

5. Alicia Rodriguez
   24-68 82 St.
   Elmhurst, N.Y. 11122

COLUMN II

Ms. Joan Kielly
318 Franklin Ave.
Brooklyn, N.Y. 11202

Mrs. Ellen Engel
47-24 86 Road
Queens, New York 11122

Marcia Michaels
213 E. 81 St.
New York, N.Y. 10012

Rev. Edward J. Smyth
1401 Brandies Street
San Francisco, Calif. 96201

Alicia Rodriguez
2468 81 St.
Elmhurst, N.Y. 11122

1.____

2.____

3.____

4.____

5.____

2 (#1)

COLUMN I	COLUMN II	
6. Ernest Eisemann 21 Columbia St. New York, N.Y. 10007	Ernest Eisermann 21 Columbia St. New York, N.Y. 10007	6._____
7. Mr. & Mrs. George Petersson 87-11 91st Avenue Woodhaven, N.Y. 11421	Mr. & Mrs. George Peterson 87-11 91st Avenue Woodhaven, N.Y. 11421	7._____
8. Mr. Ivan Klebnikov 1848 Newkirk Avenue Brooklyn, N.Y. 11226	Mr. Ivan Klebikov 1848 Newkirk Avenue Brooklyn, N.Y. 11622	8._____
9. Mr. Samuel Rothfleisch 71 Pine Street New York, N.Y. 10005	Samuel Rothfleisch 71 Pine Street New York, N.Y. 100005	9._____
10. Mrs. Isabel Tonnessen 198 East 185th Street Bronx, N.Y. 10458	Mrs. Isabel Tonnessen 189 East 185th Street Bronx, N.Y. 10348	10._____
11. Esteban Perez 173 Eighth Street Staten Island, N.Y. 10306	Estaban Perez 173 Eighth Street Staten Island, N.Y. 10306	11._____
12. Esta Wong 141 West 68 St. New York, N.Y. 10023	Esta Wang 141 West 68 St. New York, N.Y. 10023	12._____
13. Dr. Alberto Grosso 3475 12th Avenue Brooklyn, N.Y. 11218	Dr. Alberto Grosso 3475 12th Avenue Brooklyn, N.Y. 11218	13._____
14. Mrs. Ruth Bortias 482 Theresa Ct. Far Rockaway, N.Y. 11691	Ms. Ruth Bortlas 482 Theresa Ct. Far Rockaway, N.Y. 11169	14._____
15. Mr. & Mrs. Howard Fox 2301 Sedgwick Ave. Bronx, N.Y. 10468	Mr. & Mrs. Howard Fox 231 Sedgwick Ave. Bronx, N.Y. 10468	15._____
16. Miss Marjorie Black 223 East 23 Street New York, N.Y. 10010	Miss Margorie Black 223 East 23 Street New York, N.Y. 10010	16._____

3 (#1)

<u>COLUMN I</u>　　　　　　　　　　　　<u>COLUMN II</u>

17.　Michelle Herman　　　　　　　　Michelle Hermann　　　　　　　　17.____
　　 806 Valley Rd.　　　　　　　　　 806 Valley Dr.
　　 Old Tappan, N.J. 07675　　　　　Old Tappan, N.J. 07675

KEY (CORRECT ANSWERS)

1.	C	7.	A	13.	D
2.	A	8.	C	14.	C
3.	D	9.	D	15.	B
4.	B	10.	B	16.	A
5.	B	11.	A	17.	C
6.	A	12.	D		

TEST 2

DIRECTIONS: Questions 1 through 15 are to be answered SOLELY on the instructions given below. *PRINT THE LETTER OF THE CORRECT ANSWER IN THE SPACE AT THE RIGHT.*

INSTRUCTIONS

In each of the following questions, the 3-line name and address in Column I is the master-list entry, and the 3-line entry in Column II is the information to be checked against the master list. If there is one line that does not match, mark your answer A; if there are two lines that do not match, mark your answer B; if all three lines do not match, mark your answer C; if the lines all match exactly, mark your answer D.

Sample Question

Column I
Mark L. Field
11-09 Price Park Blvd.
Bronx, N.Y. 11402

Column II
Mark L. Field
11-99 Prince Park Way
Bronx, N.Y. 11401

The first lines in each column match exactly. The second lines do not match since 11-09 does not match 11-99; and Blvd. does not match Way. The third lines do not match either since 11402 does not match 11401. Therefore, there are two lines that do not match, and the CORRECT answer is B.

COLUMN I

1. Jerome A. Jackson
   1243 14th Avenue
   New York, N.Y. 10023

2. Sophie Strachtheim
   33-28 Connecticut Ave.
   Far Rockaway, N.Y. 11697

3. Elisabeth N.T. Gorrell
   256 Exchange St.
   New York, N.Y. 10013

4. Maria J. Gonzalez
   7516 E. Sheepshead Rd.
   Brooklyn, N.Y. 11240

5. Leslie B. Brautenweiler
   21 57A Seiler Terr.
   Flushing, N.Y. 11367

COLUMN II

Jerome A. Johnson
1234 14th Avenue
New York, N.Y. 10023

Sophie Strachtheim
33-28 Connecticut Ave.
Far Rockaway, N.Y. 11697

Elizabeth N.T. Gorrell
256 Exchange St.
New York, N.Y. 10013

Maria J. Gonzalez
7516 N. Shepshead Rd.
Brooklyn, N.Y. 11240

Leslie B. Brautenwieler
21-75A Seiler Terr.
Flushing, N.J. 11367

1.____

2.____

3.____

4.____

5.____

2 (#2)

	COLUMN I	COLUMN II	
6.	Rigoberto J. Peredes 157 Twin Towers, #18F Tottenville, S. I., N.Y,	Rigoberto J. Peredes 157 Twin Towers, #18F Tottenville, S.I., N.Y.	6.____
7.	Pietro F. Albino P.O. Box 7548 Floral Park, N.Y. 11005	Pietro F. Albina P.O. Box 7458 Floral Park, N.Y. 11005	7.____
8.	Joanne Zimmerman Bldg. SW, Room 314 532-4601	Joanne Zimmermann Bldg. SW, Room 314 532-4601	8.____
9.	Carlyle Whetstone Payroll Div. –A, Room 212A 262-5000, ext. 471	Carlyle Whetstone Payroll Div. –A, Room 212A 262-5000, ext. 417	9.____
10.	Kenneth Chiang Legal Council, Room 9745 (201) 416-9100, ext. 17	Kenneth Chiang Legal Counsel, Room 9745 (201) 416-9100, Ext. 17	10.____
11.	Ethel Koenig Personnel Services Division, Room 433; 635-7572	Ethel Hoenig Personal Services Division, Room 433; 635-7527	11.____
12.	Joyce Ehrhardt Office of the Administrator, Room W56; 387-8706	Joyce Ehrhart Office of the Administrator, Room W56; 387-7806	12.____
13.	Ruth Lang EAM Bldg., Room C101 625-2000, ext. 765	Ruth Lang EAM Bldg., Room C110 625-2000, ext. 765	13.____
14.	Anne Marie Ionozzi Investigations, Room 827 576-4000, ext. 832	Anna Marie Ionozzi Investigation, Room 827 566-4000, ext. 832	14.____
15.	Willard Jameson Fm C Bldg., Room 687 454-3010	Willard Jamieson Fm C Bldg., Room 687 454-3010	15.____

KEY (CORRECT ANSWERS)

1.	B	6.	D	11.	C
2.	D	7.	B	12.	B
3.	A	8.	D	13.	A
4.	A	9.	B	14.	C
5.	C	10.	A	15.	A

TEST 3

DIRECTIONS: Questions 1 through 10 are to be answered on the basis of the following instructions. *PRINT THE LETTER OF THE CORRECT ANSWER IN THE SPACE AT THE RIGHT.*

INSTRUCTIONS

For each such set of names, addresses, and numbers listed in Columns I and II, select your answer from the following options:
The names in Columns I and II are different,
The addresses in Columns I and II are different,
The numbers in Columns I and II are different,
The names, addresses, and numbers in Columns I and II are identical.

	COLUMN I	COLUMN II	
1.	Francis Jones 62 Stately Avenue 96-12446	Francis Jones 62 Stately Avenue 96-21446	1._____
2.	Julio Montez 19 Ponderosa Road 56-73161	Julio Montez 19 Ponderosa Road 56-71361	2._____
3.	Mary Mitchell 2314 Melbourne Drive 68-92172	Mary Mitchell 2314 Melbourne Drive 68-92172	3._____
4.	Harry Patterson 25 Dunne Street 14-33430	Harry Patterson 25 Dunne Street 14-34330	4._____
5.	Patrick Murphy 171 West Hosmer Street 93-81214	Patrick Murphy 171 West Hosmer Street 93-18214	5._____
6.	August Schultz 816 St. Clair Avenue 53-40149	August Schultz 816 St. Claire Avenue 53-40149	6._____
7.	George Taft 72 Runnymede Street 47-04033	George Taft 72 Runnymede Street 47-04023	7._____
8.	Angus Henderson 1418 Madison Street 81-76375	Angus Henderson 1318 Madison Street 81-76375	8._____

2 (#3)

COLUMN I	COLUMN II	
9. Carolyn Mazur 12 Riverview Road 38-99615	Carolyn Mazur 12 Rivervane Road 38-99615	9.____
10. Adele Russell 1725 Lansing Lane 72-91962	Adela Russell 1725 Lansing Lane 72-91962	10.____

KEY (CORRECT ANSWERS)

1. C 6. B
2. C 7. C
3. D 8. D
4. C 9. B
5. C 10. A

TEST 4

DIRECTIONS: Questions 1 through 20 test how good you are at catching mistakes in typing or printing. In each question, the name and address in Column II should be an exact copy of the name and address in Column I. Mark your answer
A. If there is no mistake in either name or address;
B. If there is a mistake in both name and address;
C. If there is a mistake only in the name;
D. If there is a mistake only in the address.

PRINT THE LETTER OF THE CORRECT ANSWER IN THE SPACE AT THE RIGHT.

COLUMN I | COLUMN II

1. Milos Yanocek
33-60 14 Street
Long Island City, N.Y. 11011

    Milos Yanocek
33-60 14 Street
Long Island City, N.Y. 11001

    1.____

2. Alphonse Sabattelo
24 Minnetta Lane
New York, N.Y. 10006

    Alphonse Sabbattelo
24 Minetta Lane
New York, N.Y. 10006

    2.____

3. Helen Steam
5 Metropolitan Oval
Bronx, N.Y. 10462

    Helene Stearn
5 Metropolitan Oval
Bronx, N.Y. 10462

    3.____

4. Jacob Weisman
231 Francis Lewis Boulevard
Forest Hills, N.Y. 11325

    Jacob Weisman
231 Francis Lewis Boulevard
Forest Hills, N.Y. 11325

    4.____

5. Riccardo Fuente
134 West 83 Street
New York, N.Y. 10024

    Riccardo Fuentes
134 West 88 Street
New York, N.Y. 10024

    5.____

6. Dennis Lauber
52 Avenue D
Brooklyn, N.Y. 11216

    Dennis Lauder
52 Avenue D
Brooklyn, N.Y. 11216

    6.____

7. Paul Cutter
195 Galloway Avenue
Staten Island, N.Y. 10356

    Paul Cutter
175 Galloway Avenue
Staten Island, N.Y. 10365

    7.____

8. Sean Donnelly
45-58 41 Avenue
Woodside, N.Y. 11168

    Sean Donnelly
45-58 41 Avenue
Woodside, N.Y. 11168

    8.____

9. Clyde Willot
1483 Rockaway Avenue
Brooklyn, N.Y. 11238

    Clyde Willat
1483 Rockaway Avenue
Brooklyn, N.Y. 11238

    9.____

2 (#4)

COLUMN I	COLUMN II	
10. Michael Stanakis 419 Sheriden Avenue Staten Island, N.Y. 10363	Michael Stanakis 419 Sheraden Avenue Staten Island, N.Y. 10363	10.____
11. Joseph DiSilva 63-84 Saunders Road Rego Park, N.Y. 11431	Joseph Disilva 64-83 Saunders Road Rego Park, N.Y. 11431	11.____
12. Linda Polansky 2224 Fendon Avenue Bronx, N.Y. 20464	Linda Polansky 2255 Fenton Avenue Bronx, N.Y. 10464	12.____
13. Alfred Klein 260 Hillside Terrace Staten Island, N.Y. 15545	Alfred Klein 260 Hillside Terrace Staten Island, N.Y. 15545	13.____
14. William McDonnell 504 E. 55 Street New York, N.Y. 10103	William McConnell 504 E. 55 Street New York, N.Y. 10108	14.____
15. Angela Cipolla 41-11 Parson Avenue Flushing, N.Y. 11446	Angela Cipola 41-11 Parsons Avenue Flushing, N.Y. 11446	15.____
16. Julie Sheridan 1212 Ocean Avenue Brooklyn, N.Y. 11237	Julia Sheridan 1212 Ocean Avenue Brooklyn, N.Y. 11237	16.____
17. Arturo Rodriguez 2156 Cruger Avenue Bronx, N.Y. 10446	Arturo Rodrigues 2156 Cruger Avenue Bronx, N.Y. 10446	17.____
18. Helen McCabe 2044 East 19 Street Brooklyn, N.Y. 11204	Helen McCabe 2040 East 19 Street Brooklyn, N.Y. 11204	18.____
19. Charles Martin 526 West 160 Street New York, N.Y. 10022	Charles Martin 526 West 160 Street New York, N.Y. 10022	19.____
20. Morris Rabinowitz 31 Avenue M Brooklyn, N.Y. 11216	Morris Rabinowitz 31 Avenue N Brooklyn, N.Y. 11216	20.____

KEY (CORRECT ANSWERS)

1.	D	11.	B
2.	B	12.	D
3.	C	13.	A
4.	A	14.	B
5.	B	15.	B
6.	C	16.	C
7.	D	17.	C
8.	A	18.	D
9.	B	19.	A
10.	D	20.	D

TEST 5

DIRECTIONS: In copying the addresses below from Column A to the same line in Column B, an Agent-in-Training made some errors. For Questions 1 through 5, if you find that the agent made an error in
only one line, mark your answer A;
only two lines, mark your answer B;
only three lines, mark your answer C;
all four lines, mark your answer D.

EXAMPLE

COLUMN A	COLUMN B
24 Third Avenue	24 Third Avenue
5 Lincoln Road	5 Lincoln Street
50 Central Park West	6 Central Park West
37-21 Queens Boulevard	21-37 Queens Boulevard

Since errors were made on only three lines, namely the second, third, and fourth, the CORRECT answer is C.
PRINT THE LETTER OF THE CORRECT ANSWER IN THE SPACE AT THE RIGHT.

COLUMN A	COLUMN B
1. 57-22 Springfield Boulevard 94 Gun Hill Road 8 New Dorp Lane 36 Bedford Avenue	75-22 Springfield Boulevard 94 Gun Hill Avenue 8 New Drop Lane 36 Bedford Avenue
2. 538 Castle Hill Avenue 54-15 Beach Channel Drive 21 Ralph Avenue 162 Madison Avenue	538 Castle Hill Avenue 54-15 Beach Channel Drive 21 Ralph Avenue 162 Morrison Avenue
3. 49 Thomas Street 27-21 Northern Blvd. 86 125th Street 872 Atlantic Ave.	49 Thomas Street 21-27 Northern Blvd. 86 125th Street 872 Baltic Ave,
4. 261-17 Horace Harding Expwy. 191 Fordham Road 6 Victory Blvd. 552 Oceanic Ave.	261-17 Horace Harding Pkwy. 191 Fordham Road 6 Victoria Blvd. 552 Ocean Ave.
5. 90-05 38th Avenue 19 Central Park West 9281 Avenue X 22 West Farms Square	90-05 36th Avenue 19 Central Park East 9281 Avenue X 22 West Farms Square

1.____
2.____
3.____
4.____
5.____

KEY (CORRECT ANSWERS)

1. C
2. A
3. B
4. C
5. B

TEST 6

DIRECTIONS: For Questions 1 through 10, choose the letter in Column II next to the number which EXACTLY matches the number in Column I. *PRINT THE LETTER OF THE CORRECT ANSWER IN THE SPACE AT THE RIGHT.*

COLUMN I   COLUMN II

1. 14235
   - A. 13254
   - B. 12435
   - C. 13245
   - D. 14235

   1.____

2. 70698
   - A. 90768
   - B. 60978
   - C. 70698]
   - D. 70968

   2.____

3. 11698
   - A. 11689
   - B. 11986
   - C. 11968
   - D. 11698

   3.____

4. 50497
   - A. 50947
   - B. 50497
   - C. 50749
   - D. 54097

   4.____

5. 69635
   - A. 60653
   - B. 69630
   - C. 69365
   - D. 69635

   5.____

6. 1201022011
   - A. 1201022011
   - B. 1201020211
   - C. 1202012011
   - D. 1021202011

   6.____

7. 3893981389
   - A. 3893891389
   - B. 3983981389
   - C. 3983891389
   - D. 3893981389

   7.____

8. 4765476589
   - A. 4765476598
   - B. 4765476588
   - C. 4765476589
   - D. 4765746589

   8.____

9. 8679678938
    A. 8679687938
    B. 8679678938
    C. 8697678938
    D. 8678678938

    9.____

10. 6834836932
    A. 6834386932
    B. 6834836923
    C. 6843836932
    D. 6834836932

    10.____

Questions 11-15.

DIRECTIONS: For Questions 11 through 15, determine how many of the symbols in Column Z are exactly the same as the symbol in Column Y.
If none is exactly the same, answer A;
If only one symbol is exactly the same, answer B;
If two symbols are exactly the same, answer C;
If three symbols are exactly the same, answer D.

COLUMN Y | COLUMN Z

11. A123B1266

    A123B1366
    A123B1266
    A133B1366
    A123B1266

    11.____

12. CC28D3377

    CD22D3377
    CC38D3377
    CC28C3377
    CC28D2277

    12.____

13. M21AB201X

    M12AB201X
    M21AB201X
    M21AB201Y
    M21BA201X

    13.____

14. PA383Y744

    AP383Y744
    PA338Y744
    PA388Y744
    PA383Y774

    14.____

15. PB2Y8893

    PB2Y8893
    PB2Y8893
    PB3Y8898
    PB2Y8893

    15.____

KEY (CORRECT ANSWERS)

1.	D	6.	A	11.	C
2.	C	7.	D	12.	A
3.	D	8.	C	13.	B
4.	B	9.	B	14.	A
5.	D	10.	D	15.	D

EXAMINATION SECTION
TEST 1

DIRECTIONS: Each question or incomplete statement is followed by several suggested answers or completions. Select the one that BEST answers the question or completes the statement. *PRINT THE LETTER OF THE CORRECT ANSWER IN THE SPACE AT THE RIGHT.*

1. A DMV clerk is assisting a customer who is seeking to renew his driver's license. The customer becomes agitated and confrontational over how long it is taking. Which of the following would be the BEST response for a positive outcome in this situation?
   A. Tell the customer to leave and come back when he is in a better mood
   B. Attempt to de-escalate the situation while also efficiently completing the renewal
   C. Explain that policy does not allow the workers to move any faster
   D. See if another employee can take over while avoiding direct contact with the hostile customer

   1.____

2. A village employee fields a call and question about an upcoming event at Town Hall for which he does not know the answer.
   Which is the BEST response for him to make?
   A. "Great question; let me find that out for you right now!"
   B. "Oh that is a good question...I don't know."
   C. "You need to call back later when a supervisor can answer your question."
   D. "What a good question! Unfortunately, I'm new here and don't know all of the policies. If you call back in a few days I should be able to help."

   2.____

3. A customer walks into the post office and wants to buy the new limited-edition collectible stamps, but they were not shipped on time so the postal clerk will not have them for another few days.
   What should the clerk do to remedy this situation?
   A. Tell the customer the stamps are back-ordered and that he cannot provide any further assistance on the matter
   B. Apologize and offer to give the customer a list of phone numbers for regional post offices to see if they have the stamps
   C. Apologize for the delay and give the customer the specific date that the stamps will be available
   D. Tell the customer the post office operates on a first-come, first-serve basis and she'll have to check back each day if she wants to make sure they received the stamps

   3.____

4. A translator for the Department of Justice receives a call from someone seeking information about one of his family members, but is unable to fully meet the needs of the caller because of the translator's unfamiliarity with the speaker's dialect.

   4.____

How should the translator handle this situation?
- A. "Sir, I am sorry but I'm going to have to transfer you to someone else."
- B. "Hi, sorry to interrupt, but you will need to call back with someone who can speak a little more clearly."
- C. "Hello, just to be clear, I am having a lot of trouble understanding you. Would you mind if I transfer you to someone else?"
- D. "Hello, Mr. [Last Name]! Let's get this problem resolved for you. I'm going to transfer you to a senior linguist that specializes in your specific dialect. They will be able to best aid you."

5. A doctor for the Department of Veterans Affairs is working with a patient who asks her to prescribe some extra medication to help with his pain. The doctor has already given him the appropriate amount.
What should the doctor do?
- A. Explain that as much as she'd like to fulfill the patient's request, the medication policy in place is too important as it deals with the patient's safety and health
- B. Ignore the request and pretend as though she didn't hear the patient
- C. Give the patient the medication if he obviously needs it for pain management
- D. Report the patient to the police and have him arrested for attempting to possess controlled substances

6. A local resident comes into Village Hall upset because someone issued him the wrong permit for a deck renovation on his house.
As someone who did NOT issue the permit, how should the employee handle this situation?
- A. Ask the resident to show proof of the wrong permit and then ask what permit he should have
- B. Explain to the resident that it could not have been the fault of the Village Hall employee and that he [the resident] must have submitted the wrong application
- C. Tell the resident how sorry he is that this happened, attempt to explain what could have happened and then resolve the situation by approving the correct permit
- D. Find out who issued the wrong permit and explain that the employee was wrong, then find the employee and have them fix their mistake

7. A local park district that recently joined Twitter has received public backlash from its residents due to poor communication. In one specific instance, a children's art class was canceled, but the park district did not announce it until after the event would have started and did not offer refunds.
How should the person in charge of the Twitter account respond to angry residents who have complained about the lack of communication?
- A. Tell them to contact the park district anytime between 9 A.M. and 5 P.M., which are the normal operating hours
- B. Post a silly meme that makes fun of the park district's slow response and also acts as an apology

C. Put out a message that apologizes for tardiness, assures better communication and offers a discount on future programs
D. Tweet out an offer of a partial refund (for the missed class), a sincere apology and a promise to communicate better going forward

8. A postal employee overhears a customer at the post office make the following statement to a co-worker who has Chinese ancestry: "Are you Shu? Or Mou? I can never tell you guys apart!" The customer seems jovial and not angry, but it is clear the co-worker is bothered by this interaction.
What should the employee do?
    A. Yell at the customer and tell him to come back when he is not so racist
    B. Take over for the co-worker and explain to the customer that she would be glad to help, but only on the basis of mutual respect
    C. Attempt to explain to the customer that his joke is prejudiced and unacceptable
    D. Ignore the situation and try to comfort the co-worker after the customer has left

8.____

9. A female Village Hall clerk has been working with a resident all day and has built up a rapport with him while assisting with his issue. As their business starts to conclude, the resident asks if the clerk would like to grab a bite to eat or some coffee after they're done for the day. The clerk is uncomfortable and unsure of what to do.
How should she respond?
    A. "Oh, I'm so tired and I think someone else can handle the rest of your business today."
    B. "That is thoughtful of you, but I'd like to keep this professional and focus on finishing up our business here."
    C. "I suppose we could grab a small bite to eat before I head home."
    D. "Please do not ask me out on a date! You are completely out of line!"

9.____

10. A participant in one of the town-run youth leagues broke his arm two days before the league was set to kick off. Because of the injury, he will be unable to participate, so the boy's mother asks the youth league director for a refund. The mother signed a waiver that clearly states that no refunds can be issued for the league within a week of it starting. Despite this, she asks for an exception because of the circumstance.
What should the league director do?
    A. Attempt to explain why the policy is the way it is, show he understands the frustration of the parent, but reiterate that nothing can be done
    B. Empathize with the parent and show agreement with her, but explain that is not something that can be changed by one person and promise to take this to a superior to solve the issue
    C. Make it clear that an alternative to the policy will be sought, offer another league or activity that the boy could be a part of, or waive the cost of the league for the next year
    D. Explain that the boy and parent should have been more aware of activities that might cause injury and share educational materials on injury prevention and rehabilitation

10.____

11. An employee that works for the state's tourism department receives a phone call from a potential tourist asking for information about attractions. As he starts to answer, the caller interrupts, asks inappropriate questions, and seems to be trying to frustrate the employee.
    How should this situation be handled?
    A. He should play it cool by explaining that they would love to answer any actual questions if the caller is being sincere, and if insincere, explain that he needs to attend to other callers who have legitimate questions
    B. He should stay civil and answer all questions the caller has
    C. He should become aggressive and rude back to the caller before hanging up
    D. He should tell the caller he will be right back, but leave the caller on hold indefinitely

11.____

12. An employee in the Citizen Service and Response Department for a town in Virginia handles non-emergency citizen service requests. Recently, the employee received praise via Twitter for an expedient solution to a child's need, but the employee was not the one who actually solved the citizen's problem.
    What should she do?
    A. Denounce the tweet as false and tweet about the person who deserves the praise
    B. Take credit for the tweet, but be sure to mention others that were involved
    C. Reach out to the citizen outside of social media and explain who the real hero was
    D. Express gratitude for the recognition, but highlight the coworker who was truly responsible

12.____

13. A resident complains to you that your facility is making exaggerated and false claims about the benefits of joining their exercise classes. She wants you to immediately take down the advertisement and publicly apologize for misleading the community.
    What should you do?
    A. Refer her to your supervisor – this is well above your pay grade
    B. Act like you are interested, but dismiss the resident's claim as crazy and does not warrant taking action
    C. Listen with an open mind and determine if there is any truth to the resident's claims. Make a promise to look into the matter, but do not commit to changing anything.
    D. Immediately take down the advertisement and issue the apology. Residents' tax dollars are responsible for the funding you receive, so you cannot risk angering them.

13.____

14. A customer becomes confused as to which line he is supposed to be on at the DMV. After a lengthy wait, the man arrives at your station for a driver's license renewal, but you explain you are working on license-plate services only. He slumps his shoulders and displays some distress before imploring you to make an exception for him so he does not have to go back to the end of the line and start all over.
    What should you do?
    A. Tell him you would love to help, but going against policy could negatively impact your performance review
    B. Garner the attention of your co-worker who is working license renewals and have him put the customer higher up in his queue
    C. Repeat your initial statement that he is in the wrong line, then ignore his request and ask for the next customer in line
    D. Leave your post and have the customer follow. Explain the situation to your co-worker working at license renewal and have the customer jump to the front of the line.

14.____

15. A Village Hall employee is talking on the phone with a resident who needs help registering for a program electronically, but during the discussion the employee realizes the resident is not at home and does not have access to necessary registration information.
    How should the employee proceed?
    A. Direct the customer to look for the answer on the village's website when she is at home
    B. Hang up on the caller – obviously, she does not know what she is doing and does not deserve the help
    C. Tell the customer that she cannot be helped until she has the correct information, then end the call
    D. Establish a time for the person to call back when she is able to provide the relevant information

15.____

16. An employee at the Recreational Center receives a phone call from a resident who says, "I am very upset that my meeting with your service director did not start at the appointed time. I was told the meeting would start at 11:30 A.M. and he did not arrive until 12:15 P.M. I took the morning off from work to make this meeting, but I did not need to if I had known the meeting was going to be so late!" After politely putting the person on hold, the employee calls the director who tells her the meeting began late because of heavy traffic and a previous meeting that had run long.
    Once the employee takes the resident off hold, how should she respond?
    A. Offer sincere apologies and explain what happened without making excuses for the late start to the meeting
    B. Apologize profusely to the resident, but give the contact information for the director, so the director can explain what happened
    C. Tell the resident that sometimes meetings run late and that she could have left if she wanted to, as it was a voluntary meeting
    D. Ask the resident what she would like the employee to do about the situation

16.____

17. An elderly customer calls the post office with a problem finding some product information on the website. He is polite yet frustrated and upset that he cannot find the information he is seeking. The post office employee recognizes what the elderly man is looking for, but realizes the information is too long and complicated to share over the phone.
    What are the BEST steps for the employee to take?
    A. Tell him he can find the information he is looking for in the product information section of the website
    B. Offer to find the specific information he needs and e-mail it to him directly
    C. Advise him to go to the product information section of the website and print out all of the available material so that he can review it offline
    D. Send him a link to a video tutorial that shows customers how to navigate the post office website

18. A DMV clerk is attempting to explain procedures to a customer that seems to be hard of hearing. The clerk explains twice, but the customer does not seem to understand.
    What should the clerk do?
    A. Explain that he is not sure what the customer does not understand and walk away
    B. Ask someone else to help the customer
    C. Repeat the procedures for the third time and try to explain it slightly differently or with written instructions
    D. Repeat the procedures for the third time and then ask for the next customer in line

19. A resident is considering signing up for a fitness program through the park district, though the trainer running the program knows it will not completely fulfill the customer's needs.
    What should the trainer do?
    A. Alert the resident to what the program will actually cover and explain that it is still worth the customer's time even if it doesn't fully meet what he is looking for
    B. Answer any questions the customer may have, but do nothing else, as the trainer can support the customer after they've started
    C. Suggest that a non-district fitness program might be better and offer to find the information for him
    D. Make any promises and guarantees about the program that is needed. Once he signs up, the customer is not the employee's concern anymore.

20. A resident comes into a county clerk's office looking upset and distraught. How can the clerk display active listening skills so the resident can at least know that her voice was heard?
    A. Nod and make eye contact as the resident tells her story
    B. Frequently ask the resident if she would like any water or snacks while she tells her story
    C. Use phrases like "I see" or "Go on" whenever it seems to be an appropriate pause
    D. Both A and C

21. A public defense attorney meets with a client who becomes aggressive and combative when the attorney asks for clarification on an event that the client was a part of.
How should the attorney respond?
   A. Change his behavior in various ways to get the best possible outcome
   B. Mirror the client's behavior, becoming frustrated and aggressive
   C. Walk out of the meeting. If the client will not respect the attorney, then why should the attorney respect the client?
   D. None of the above

21.____

22. A very important resident of your village contacts your department and is upset about the way one of your co-workers handled the processing of his permit application.
Which of the following is the BEST way to move forward with this situation?
   A. Rush to respond to him right away as he is very important and busy
   B. Take responsibility for the mix-up and attempt to figure out how to appropriately fix the issue
   C. Attempt to see why he is so antagonistic and suggest he is part of the problem
   D. Make promises about fixing the issue as promptly as possible, even if you cannot actually keep the promise

22.____

23. An administrative assistant for the local police station receives a phone call from an angry resident. The assistant wants to aid in resolving the resident's issue and calm her down before she talks to an officer.
Which of the following steps should the assistant take while talking to the resident?
   A. Empathize   B. Diagnose
   C. Apologize   D. All of the above

23.____

24. After an ice storm passed through the area, the steps outside of Village Hall iced over. While an employee attempted to salt the area outside the building, a person slipped and fell as they were attempting to come in for a meeting.
How should this situation be handled?
   A. Start gathering evidence to prove that reasonable attempts were made to prevent injury for customers walking into the building
   B. Call insurance to get a claims adjustor out to the building as fast as possible to assist the person
   C. Get immediate medical attention for the person who is injured
   D. None of the above

24.____

25. A local customer of the park district tweets in his Twitter account poking fun at how slow and behind the times the park district is. After a week, the comments do not seem to stop.
Which of the following should the park district NOT do regarding the customer and his tweets?
    A. Directly contact the Twitter user to see what ways the park district could improve their slow process
    B. Before responding, check to ensure the response is professional and courteous
    C. Censor the Twitter account responsible for the tweet
    D. The park district should avoid doing all of the things mentioned above

KEY (CORRECT ANSWERS)

1.	B		11.	A
2.	A		12.	D
3.	C		13.	C
4.	D		14.	B
5.	A		15.	D
6.	C		16.	A
7.	D		17.	B
8.	B		18.	C
9.	B		19.	A
10.	C		20.	D

21.	A
22.	B
23.	D
24.	C
25.	C

TEST 2

DIRECTIONS: Each question or incomplete statement is followed by several suggested answers or completions. Select the one that BEST answers the question or completes the statement. *PRINT THE LETTER OF THE CORRECT ANSWER IN THE SPACE AT THE RIGHT.*

1. Recently, the village mayor made controversial statements that angered many of the local residents. An employee at Village Hall has received a call from one of these angry people.
   How should she handle this situation?
   A. Deny any knowledge of the situation and explain that it is not her job to comment on the mayor's opinions
   B. Apologize and be transparent about what happened
   C. Give the person the mayor's phone number at Village Hall and explain they should be talking to the mayor
   D. Once the employee realizes what the phone call is about, she should see if there is any constructive criticism to bring to the mayor and promise to do so

1.____

2. A local patron comes into the library and claims that he was charged for not returning a book that he says was returned to the drop box after the library was closed. The librarian knows that the patron never returned the book and is just trying to avoid paying the fine for a lost book.
   Which of the following statements should she make to the patron?
   A. "Sir, I know you're frustrated and I completely empathize. My goal is to help you sort this out."
   B. "Listen, I know you lost the book and you know you lost the book, so let's stop playing games and you can pay your fine if you wish to continue to check out books here."
   C. "Sir, I am so sorry that this happened! I know we'll get to the bottom of this – and that starts with your being honest about the book."
   D. "Sir, I tell you what. Do not worry about it. I am sure the book was returned and we just misplaced it. I'll wipe the fine and you can go ahead and check out any books you wish."

2.____

3. A resident calls the park district fitness center to cancel her membership.
   What should the employee who receives the call do?
   A. Attempt to convince the resident to keep her membership by promoting the health benefits of an active lifestyle
   B. Keep the resident on the line and attempt to have her join another activity such as a league or tennis lessons
   C. Apologize that the fitness center could not fit her needs, cancel the membership, and ask what went wrong so the center can improve in the future.
   D. Cancel the membership and promptly hang up

3.____

4. The local post office receives a phone call from an angry customer who wants to know why her package has not yet arrived. Upon checking the tracking for the package, the employee cannot determine where the package is.
   How should he proceed?
   A. Apologize for the package not arriving on time
   B. Admit that as of right now the package cannot be located
   C. Explain the process for filing a claim on a missing or lost package
   D. All of the above

   4.____

5. An IRS employee recently received training on how to comply with equality legislation when a customer calls asking for assistance on a tax issue they're having.
   How should this recent training affect that phone call?
   A. Range of services will decrease   B. Service offer will be limited
   C. Fair service will be provided   D. Range of services will increase

   5.____

6. A customer attempts to reach out to the Public Works Department of her local government via Twitter to ask a question about garbage collection. The Public Works main Twitter account informs the customer that she will need to contact the Garbage Collection Twitter account in order for her question to be answered. The customer is frustrated because of how long it is taking for her to receive a simple answer.
   How could Public Works improve in the future to improve its social media customer service?
   A. Assess the need for multiple accounts for the department, as it could be better to have one social media platform with shared ownership between departments
   B. Educate each department's social media team on how to provide the best possible customer care via social media
   C. Ask customers to contact the department by more conventional means in order to better handle customer service
   D. Both A and B

   6.____

7. An irate resident telephones a clerk who handles housing tax assessments for the town.
   How should the clerk react so that the customer's expectations are met with a positive outcome?
   A. Follow the department's procedures for this kind of call
   B. Describe why the issue happened
   C. Urge the resident to be more patient since there are new members on department staff
   D. Support the department's position and tell the resident to submit his complaint in writing

   7.____

8. A concerned citizen is following up on a report she made to Child and Youth Services two days ago.
   What should the employee receiving the citizen's follow-up do to make sure the situation is handled effectively?

   8.____

A. Issue the full report to the citizen
B. Express gratitude for filing a report and explain that Child and Youth Services takes it very seriously and is looking into the matter. Tell her that it is the policy of Child and Youth Services to not discuss open or closed investigations with citizens.
C. Explain to the citizen that the report has been filed and the situation has been taken care of, and that she should follow up with the child's family for specific details
D. None of the above

9. When a resident asks why Village Hall needs him to fill out an online survey he just received, what should the employee's explanation be?
    A. So organizational procedure changes can be avoided
    B. So changes can be made to ensure and maintain resident satisfaction
    C. So residents can be added to a list that informs of upcoming events
    D. So information can be gathered and shared with other organizations and departments

10. Someone walks into the local Health Department looking to talk to anyone who works there. The employee who helps her has no knowledge of the person or the meeting ahead of time.
    What question should the employee ask to help establish the person's needs?
    A. "Are you happy with how you've been treated so far?"
    B. "Would you be willing to fill out a survey after this to attest to the great care and service you received today?"
    C. "I would love to help you, but I do not know what you need yet."
    D. "Is there anything I can help you with today?"

11. A teenager who recently passed her driving test seems very nervous when she approaches the DMV employee who will process her request.
    What technique can the employee use to help put the teen at ease?
    A. Ask the teen to hurry up
    B. Avoid speaking to the teen beyond what is necessary to process her request as quickly and efficiently as possible
    C. Relate to the teen by reminiscing about the employee's own experience
    D. Have a younger, friendlier-looking co-worker help the teen. It may put her at ease if she is closer in age.

12. During a customer interaction at the post office, an employee asks for the customer's e-mail address. The customer wants to know why they need an e-mail address.
    The employee explains that he needs the e-mail address because
    A. it will help keep customers informed of service changes, delivery delays and other pertinent information
    B. it will help increase online sales revenue through discounts and promotional offerings
    C. it allows the post office to gain more information on its customers, which it shares with the federal government
    D. all of the above

13. A man comes into the state tollway office and asks to talk to a specific employee. When he meets the employee, the person is upset because he claims the employee promised to waive fees attached to his account, but the person just received a final notice that those fees needed to be paid or further action would be taken.
    Knowing that he did make the promise, what should the employee do?
    A. Explain that the promise he made was overruled by his supervisor and that the customer must pay the fines
    B. Pretend like no promise was ever offered and tell the person he'll have to pay the fee
    C. Explain that the final notice must have been sent while the waived fees were processing, and confirm they have been removed from the account
    D. None of the above

    13.____

14. A public service employee is meeting with a local customer who is upset with how his claim has been handled.
    Which of the following should the employee AVOID doing if he wants the meeting to go well?
    A. Listen to the complaint and show empathy
    B. Take an important text/phone call during the meeting
    C. Tell the customer he will fix this issue together and solicit ideas from the customer about what he would be satisfied with
    D. Let the customer know that the employee will do everything possible to help the customer with what he needs

    14.____

15. A woman walks into the post office with a damaged package she claims she received yesterday.
    Which of the following should the employee NOT state to the woman during the ensuing conversation?
    A. "I am so sorry your product arrived damaged!"
    B. "I see your package was insured; would you like my assistance in filing an indemnity claim?"
    C. "I have had this happen to me before as well. I know how frustrated you are right now!"
    D. "Are you sure this is our fault? This doesn't look like shipping damage."

    15.____

16. The university bookstore receives a complaint from a customer who claims she bought an item there yesterday and then found it went on clearance today. What should the employee who received the customer do?
    A. Ask for the customer's item and receipt to confirm the purchase date, then credit the difference back to the customer
    B. Explain that the customer can return the item, but cannot repurchase it in order to get the discount
    C. Speak with management to ensure a credit can be given and then give it to the customer, but add that this a one-time convenience
    D. Apologize for the frustration, but explain that policy does not allow for any returns or exchanges on clearance items

    16.____

17. A dissatisfied resident engages Village Hall via Twitter to complain about the lack of quality in the road maintenance outside her house after a winter storm. How should the person in charge of social media respond to the resident's tweet?
    She should
    A. not respond, as Village Hall cannot fix every small problem and trying to respond will only call more attention to the issue
    B. tweet back for the resident to call Village Hall during normal operating hours in order to discuss the issue
    C. directly message the resident to find out why she was dissatisfied and attempt to gather feedback about a better process for fixing the issue
    D. mention the company that is contracted to handle road maintenance, so they can take care of the problem

17.____

18. An employee who is responsible for social media posts for the Parks and Recreation Department notices that a number of negative reviews recently posted about the department all seem to be made by the same online profile. After digging around, the employee determines that the profile belongs to someone who recently had a bad experience with one of the programs run by the department.
    What should the employee do?
    A. Call out the person by showing that their bad reviews are based off one experience
    B. Post a general statement about how the Parks and Recreation Department strives to give residents the best possible experience, and add that this particular resident is just "trolling"
    C. Ignore the comments and trust the public to know that one person posting negative reviews does not mean the department has a negative reputation
    D. Seek out the person privately and attempt to correct any wrongdoing on the part of the department

18.____

19. An employee for City Hall must meet with a group of concerned citizens for input on a potential City park project.
    How should the employee dress for this meeting?
    A. Dress casually because the meeting might take long
    B. Dress professionally to convey competence and ability to meet the citizens' needs
    C. Dress casually to put the citizens at ease during the meeting
    D. Dress professionally to intimidate the citizens and show superiority

19.____

20. A customer comes into the State Tollway Office and complains that he was given a defective sensor for electronic payment of tolls.
    Which of the following should the employee NOT do in his attempt to help resolve this situation?
    A. Give the customer personal contact information so he can contact the employee anytime there is an issue in the future
    B. Reimburse the customer with a new sensor

20.____

C. Compensate the customer by waiving any extra fees that may have incurred from the unprocessed tolls
D. Offer the customer a sincere apology for the inconvenience he's had to endure

21. A customer places a complicated order over the telephone. 21.____
What is the BEST way to ensure the details of the order are correct?
    A. Repeat the order over the telephone
    B. Record the telephone call
    C. Confirm the order in writing
    D. Take down the details in writing

22. There is a new initiative from Village Hall to promote a healthier lifestyle for residents, and part of the program launch features employees calling residents and then scheduling meetings to explain the initiative in greater detail. When one employee meets with a resident, the resident interrupts their original pitch and asks simply why they need to hear about the features and benefits of the program. 22.____
How should the employee respond?
    A. Kindly ask the resident to stop interrupting so he can explain everything
    B. Let the resident know that is how residents will understand what the program will do for them
    C. Explain that the village is putting such major emphasis on healthy lifestyles that it wants to discuss the benefits with residents in person
    D. Both B and C

23. A customer telephones the County Clerk's office complaining that her ADA rights are being violated because the handicapped parking space is not wide enough to accommodate her and her vehicle. The employee speaking to the customer knows that the parking space is the required 96 inches wide, but also knows that the size of a parking lot sometimes makes it difficult for customers to park correctly. 23.____
How should the employee handle this situation?
    A. Apologize to the customer and politely end the conversation. Then call the lawyer that represents the County for legal representation and counsel.
    B. Express empathy that the clerk's office is such a hassle for the customer, but explain that the building is ADA compliant. Offer to collaborate on a solution that will work for the customer.
    C. Call the customer out for being wrong. Offer to show her any forms of plans that show that the clerk's office is ADA compliant.
    D. Explain to the customer that she is right and the clerk's office will attempt to make their parking lot and handicapped spaces more compliant for the customer

24. A resident walks into the Homeowners' Association office and asks for the deadline to file an application to run for one of the offices of the HOA. The employee working does not know the answer.
What is the BEST way to respond to the resident's request?
   A. Tell the resident what she thinks the answer might be
   B. Refer the resident to a supervisor
   C. Inform the person that she does not know, but will find out as quickly as possible
   D. Explain that this kind of information is not something that can be given out to the public

25. A customer at the DMV asks an employee to do something that the employee cannot accommodate.
In responding to the request, the employee should AVOID doing which of the following?
   A. Quote DMV policy regarding the customer's request
   B. Explain to the customer why the employee cannot accommodate her request
   C. Make vague statements that allow for interpretation and, therefore, wiggle room
   D. Both A and C

KEY (CORRECT ANSWERS)

1.	B	11.	C
2.	A	12.	A
3.	C	13.	C
4.	D	14.	B
5.	C	15.	D
6.	D	16.	A
7.	A	17.	C
8.	B	18.	D
9.	B	19.	B
10.	D	20.	A

21.	A
22.	D
23.	B
24.	C
25.	D

www.ingramcontent.com/pod-product-compliance
Lightning Source LLC
Chambersburg PA
CBHW080736230426

43665CB00020B/2758